Hope for Mothers with Kids on Drugs

A Journey to Redemption

Hope
for Mothers
with Kids on Drugs

A Journey to Redemption

Leejae Morris

THE LION, THE WITCH AND THE WARDROBE by C.S. Lewis copyright © C.S. Lewis Pte. Ltd. 1950. Extract reprinted by permission.

All Scripture references are from *The Holy Bible, New Living Translation.* 2nd edition. Wheaton, Illinois: Tyndale House, 2004 unless otherwise noted.

Scriptures marked NKJV are from *The New King James Version.* (1982). Nashville: Thomas Nelson.

Scriptures marked NIV are from *The Holy Bible: New International Version.* (1984). Grand Rapids, MI: Zondervan.

Scriptures marked AMP are from *The Amplified Bible.* (1987). Grand Rapids, MI: Zondervan.

HOPE for Mothers with Kids on Drugs
A Journey to Redemption

www.MothersWithKidsOnDrugs.com

ISBN: 978-0-9998209-0-2
Publisher: Acorn Ridge Press
Printed in the United States of America
Copyright © 2018
© Cover photograph by Ken Roberge

This book is dedicated to Jesus, who loves families. He holds the hands of the mothers as they walk a path never walked before. He has mercy on the fathers whose cries are silent. He sees what our sons and daughters do and knows how they got there, but He never stops calling them to return to His open arms.

To my children, who bring joy, laughter, and love to my life.

Deepest gratitude to the prayer warriors who fought for me and my prodigal during our darkest hours – Wanda, Vernon, Cristina, Jim, Patty, Jan, Laura and Jean. Thanks to Pastors Terry and Becky who encouraged me to go forward with this book and offered their help. Special acknowledgement and thanks belong to Rory, who spent countless hours editing and improving these pages and who continually spoke uplifting words over me and the importance of taking others on this journey to healing.

CONTENTS

INTRODUCTION

I am the worst mother in the world. This is my fault. I failed as a parent. His dad said it was because I was too soft on him and this wouldn't have happened if he had raised him. A family member said it wouldn't have happened if I had kept him at a good church with a solid youth ministry instead of dragging him into a small church that suited me. It was selfish. Church kids aren't allowed to hang with him. When I walk I stare at the floor because I feel ashamed. Of me. I was the only woman I knew whose son was addicted to heroin. There was no one to talk to, no one who understood the roller coaster ride my heart was on.

If you understand and feel sure those things are being said about you, then you are one of more than 22 million mothers of the addicted in America with a child over the age of twelve battling a substance abuse disorder. You bear a burden not meant for your tender shoulders. If you say those things to yourself, sweet woman, this is not how your story has to end.

This is not a one-stop-shop, everything you wanted to know about drugs. Your child of any age may be hooked on prescription opioids, legal marijuana, alcohol or a variety of illegal street drugs. Men are more likely than women to use almost all types of illicit drugs and more men than women die from overdose. However, women are just as likely to become addicted, and they may be more susceptible to relapse. What you will read in this book applies equally to our sons and daughters. I encourage you to learn about the type of drug your child is using and how it typically affects the user. Information is helpful and now at the touch of your fingertips on the internet. Don't be afraid to educate yourself. But always remember that God's word is the absolute truth and He has the last word.

What we usually don't understand is how addiction affects us personally as well as our families. Our marriages are in trouble or dissolved. We don't understand our frozen feelings or why we can't give ourselves permission to laugh. We bury our anger and isolate ourselves more and more. Our other children may be choosing unhealthy relationships or none at all. We are all coping by not telling the truth.

Hope is necessary for your own survival. True joy can also return to your life. My story will encourage you to work on the only life you can control...your own. In the process of your own journey to healing, God is free to work miracles in the lives of all of your children.

Read it one short section at a time. Think deeply about the questions at the end. When you have answered them for yourself only, sit on it for a few days before you move on. God will reveal more about your answers at times and places you least expect.

THE LION, THE WITCH, AND THE WARDROBE
C.S. Lewis

They say Aslan is on the move---perhaps has already landed.

And now a very curious thing happened. None of the children knew who Aslan was any more than you do; but the moment the Beaver had spoken these words everyone felt quite different. Perhaps it has sometimes happened to you in a dream that someone says something which you don't understand but in the dream, it feels as if it had some enormous meaning---either a terrifying one which turns the whole dream into a nightmare or else a lovely meaning too lovely to put into words, which makes the dream so beautiful that you remember it all your life and are always wishing you could get into that dream again. It was like that now. At the name of Aslan each one of the children felt something jump in its inside. Edmund felt a sensation of mysterious horror. Peter felt suddenly brave and adventurous. Susan felt as if some delicious smell or some other delightful strain of music had just floated by her. And Lucy got the feeling you have when you wake up in the morning and realize that it is the beginning of the holidays or the beginning of summer.

CHAPTER ONE

Out of Control

He was 16 and I had known about his marijuana use for two years. I had convinced myself that the angry outbursts, school truancy, and disrespectful behavior toward me was just teenage rebellion. I did not acknowledge in my own mind that he was drinking and using drugs regularly or that his car accidents might have happened while he was high.

I did know that my life was chaotic and he needed *fixing*, so I hauled him into Dr. Wu's office. We now sat together in his small office, facing the doctor. Josh was slouched in the chair next to mine, leaning as far as he could get from me and completely silent as I railed on about his behavior. Within minutes the doctor got right to the heart of the issue. It wasn't my cocky, defiant son — it was me! What was he saying? I am the problem? Outrageous. He has missed it completely. All of my sacrifice for this boy? All the love I have poured out on him? All the money I have spent on him? If there was anyone at fault it was surely his absentee dad, not me. I could feel the anger rise in my cheeks. The good doctor was much more diplomatic than that, of course. He simply noted that my son seemed to be doing great. He was dressed in nice clothes. He went to school when he wanted to. He had a car that he didn't buy. His life seemed good. But I was angry and unhappy. I heard the words but I didn't like them or want to receive them.

Dr. Wu asked me if I was a believer.

"Yes," I said.

"Do you know the story of Eli and his sons?"

"Yes." I did, and a cold rain coursed through me.

"What happened to Eli's sons?"

"They died."

"Why?" he probed.

"Because he did nothing."

The words came out and stung my ears as I spoke them.

That knife went deep into my heart. Accusation from a doctor I barely knew. It was the Holy Spirit speaking to me through him. My son was confounded by my behavior. I would not speak to him. I was driving home like a crazy woman, angry and full of emotion. I dropped him off and went to a park with my Bible and I read about Eli.

Now Eli, who was very old, heard about everything his sons were doing to all Israel and how they slept with the women who served at the entrance to the Tent of Meeting. So he said to them, 'Why do you do such things? I hear from all the people about these wicked deeds of yours. No, my sons; it is not a good report that I hear spreading among the Lord's people. If a man sins against another man, God may mediate for him; but if

a man sins against the Lord, who will intercede for him?' His sons, however, did not listen to their father's rebuke, for it was the Lord's will to put them to death.
1 Samuel 2:22-25

Their sins were so great they were affecting an entire nation of people, and everyone saw it and talked about it. It was glaring and repulsive. Yet this fat old man didn't want to alienate his sons from him in his declining years when he might want their comfort. I read it and thought to myself, "Well, it's not like he ignored it. He called them in to talk about it."

Suddenly I saw it. Eli did what I had been doing — he *spoke* to them about their evil ways — but he lacked the courage to remove them from their role as priests — to make them suffer the consequences of their sins. The outcome for Phinehas and Hophni? *Death.* And Eli himself would fall over dead when he learned about the sudden death of his sons soon after. I had been using words and words and more words, but my son did not believe I would act on my words and they had no impact on him. He was right. O Lord, my son was going to *die* from his choices if I did nothing but speak words. I wailed alone on the park bench as God spoke to my heart. I was trying to love him and rescue him, but my love and rescuing was quickening his death. I had to love him enough to let him go.

Why then do you honor your sons before Me?
1 Samuel 2:29

What was God saying? This was the real issue of my mother-heart. When I keep a blind eye to the truth of my child's depravity or bail him out time after time — I am really saying that I can't risk him being angry with me or rejecting me when I do hard things. My inaction is saying that God isn't sufficient to meet all my needs, and I need this man, this son, this someone or something, to be complete. It was, after all, about ME! This was the hardest thing for me to see, for I had seen myself as a martyr of self-sacrificing love. But the truth is I didn't trust God with him so I continued to try to heal him with my love, which has not and will not ever be sufficient.

The next day I phoned Josh's father and asked him to come and take his son to live with him. I had been telling my son that if he did not change his ways he could not stay with me, but I never believed I would have to do it or that I had the courage to do it. That night, he ran away from home and we had to get the police to bring him out of our neighbor's garage where he was in hiding. When his father put him in his car and took him away there was hatred in my son's eyes as he glanced my way – refusing to speak to me or look directly at me. Actions not words. I was grieved and yet relieved.

We are the clay. You are the potter. We are all the work of your hands.
Isaiah 64:8

God had to wrestle him out of my hands so He could work with him and save his life. God was not so tired of my son's sin that He was ready to let him go.

Good and upright is the Lord. Therefore, he instructs sinners in **His ways**.
Psalms 25:8

God speaks to me through these verses. What are *His ways?* The same ways this loving God got my attention so many years ago. My life was in shambles and I had lost my marriage, my self-respect, my financial security, and I was at risk of losing my children. Only then did I cry out to God and say *"Change me, God. If I lose everything it's okay, but I need Jesus."*

Four years after the doctor appointment I did another hard thing. I left Josh with a duffle bag of clothes and toiletries at Haven House, 850 miles away from home for a year away from family. Three high schools, one DUI and two arrests, wrecked cars, community college failure, relocation, outpatient therapy, 2 detox units, tens of thousands of dollars, and two 28-day programs later, it had come to this – *go away* from those of us who love you too well and let us all heal. *Go away* where you can hear from God and your enablers aren't there to hug you the moment you mess up again and tell you it will be all right. *Go away* and let God save your life.

God was able to save my son's life and change his life, if I would only take my hands out of the clay and allow God to mold him and shape him into a vessel fit for use.

This is one moment in time of my son's 19 year battle with drug addiction and my own pathway to victory. Does anything in my story sound like your story? Is your hand still on the potter's wheel, believing you can mend the crack in a pot that is whirling faster than your hands can move? Be honest. Ask yourself the following questions.

Seek First to Understand

1. How many times have you rescued your son or daughter in the past year? Three years? Five years?

2. In what ways?

> Changed his school
> Kept him out of jail
> Paid his bills
> Mediated his conflicts
> Relocated him
> Other

3. How has it helped him?

4. How has it hurt him?

5. How would you describe your current emotional state?

> Calm, well-balanced
> Fragile but able to function
> Living in a constant state of fear

6. How would you describe your current health?

> No medical issues
> Frequent colds or viruses, abdominal issues, headaches, or other recurring *minor* irritations
> Under treatment for a serious health problem (cancer, rheumatoid arthritis, high blood pressure, depression)

7. How has your child's use of drugs or alcohol affected your finances in the past 3 years?

8. How has your child's use of drugs or alcohol affected your marriage, past or present?

9. Do either you or dad have a family history of substance abuse?

10. How has your child's use of drugs affected the lives of your other children?

> Are there any behavioral issues?
> Do they have healthy relationships?
> Is there any quality time with them?

If you feel overwhelmed looking at your accumulated answers you are not alone, dear one. One in six young adults age 15-26 and one in 14 adults over the age of 26 needed substance abuse treatment in 2015 in the United States. Opiates, mainly heroin, account for 18% of the hospital admissions for drug and alcohol treatment in the US. Heroin use in the United States jumped 63% between 2002 and 2013, with increases seen among men and women, most age groups, and all income levels, according to data released by the Centers for Disease Control and Prevention. 116 people died each day from opioid overdose in 2016. 10.1% of the population of the U.S. regularly uses alcohol, marijuana, prescription opioids, and/or other illicit drugs. 1.2 million people are treated in Emergency Rooms each year for crisis related to substance abuse. If the average family has five people then four other people are seriously impacted by one member's addiction. Add grandparents or step families and it's easy to see why we all *know somebody* with a serious drug or alcohol issue. The director of an opioid treatment network in the Midwest bristles at the continued use of the word *epidemic*. An epidemic lasts a few weeks, he said. This is not an epidemic but a way of life in America.

The heart of a mother feels pain that even the best of dads can't comprehend. Perhaps that's why Simeon spoke only to Mary when she and Joseph brought baby Jesus to the temple for his dedication. *"A sword will pierce through your own soul also."* It took me four years to conquer my fears and take definitive action. No matter how fearful or depressed you may feel at this moment, know that there is hope. The first step toward hope is the one you just took. You took an honest look at the situation and acknowledged that all you have done so far to help your child has not worked. Your finger is in the dyke but the flood waters are beginning to spill over the top, and no one else within shouting distance seems to know what to do either.

God's Word

I'm sticking with God. I say it over and over again — He's all I've got left. He proves to be good to me and to all who passionately wait and diligently seek Him. It's a good thing to quietly hope for help from God.
Lamentations 3:24-26 The Message

Prayer

God, I am helpless without You. I have tried and failed to save my child on my own. But I remember all the things you brought me through and all the ways you showed your love for me, and I will still place my hope in You. In Jesus. Amen

CHAPTER TWO

The Battle

Is the Lord's arm too short? You will now see whether or not what I say will come true
for you." So Moses went out and told the people what the Lord had said.
Numbers 11:23

He was 14 and there was a war going on. Not the U.S. military kind but the mother-son spiritual kind. A rock group named Korn was coming to town. *All* the kids were going. But their lyrics were about death and drugs and depression and I knew I needed to stand firm and say *No*. It set off a tirade of nose-to-nose confrontations. Back then I didn't know how to disarm the enemy. Tensions between us mounted daily as the dreaded day approached. Slammed doors and angry outbursts were followed by threats. He threatened to run away from home if I didn't let him go. I continued with my verbal *No!* but inside my heart was trembling and I wasn't sure I could keep from caving in.

A week before the concert, my best friend and I were having our Saturday morning prayer time. As we prayed on our knees about this situation, suddenly the Holy Spirit showed me that it was not just my son, but every mother's son and daughter that was under attack. No one should be going to this concert. This scripture popped into my head, *Is the Lord's arm too short?* I began to speak it out loud, requiring of God an intervention, asking Him to cancel the concert. As I spoke it, I got more bold in my request. It wasn't a pitiful, weepy prayer. It was loud and forceful, using the spiritual weapon of warfare...the Word of God. It was the heat of battle. You don't need to shout for God to hear you, but this was a shouting time for my friend and me.

The eve of the concert came. I had weakly allowed him to spend the night next door, unaware that he had already purchased a ticket with money stolen from my purse and was planning to go with the neighbors the next day and not return home. I spent that Friday night in prayer. Lord, I need an answer. I need your help. I need an intervention. Please save my son and other sons and daughters from this poison.

Saturday morning a friend from work called. "Do you have the radio on? Have you heard?" She was so excited she was shouting into the phone. No, I hadn't heard anything. "They have cancelled the Korn concert tonight! The drummer broke his arm!" To be clear, we do not curse anyone in our prayers. I didn't ask for that, but neither did I question it. Their concert tour was cancelled for several cities.

I stood in my kitchen, praising God yet also weeping, completely humbled and awed when I understood the power of prayer, the power of the Word in prayer, and the revelation that the Creator of the world turned his ear to a couple of praying women in Wentzville, Missouri, and sent His angels to do His bidding and intervene.

Josh called from next door. The group had *decided* to go to Six Flags instead of the concert. He just wanted to let me know. I held my tongue. He wouldn't understand at this time that he had a heavenly Father who reached down from the throne room for him.

Two years later I had to use that scripture again, to remind myself of God's faithfulness. He was in his father's car, backing out of the driveway, moving out of my home at my insistence. Hatred toward me was in his eyes. He wouldn't speak to me, probably couldn't for fear of what he would say. No matter what it looks like, there are days when you have to remind yourself that God's arm is not too short for any of your circumstances. He holds us close in those same arms that use the rod on our backs if we require it. It's all love.

And God loved those twisted young men in Korn. Guitarist Brian "Head" Welch of Korn received the Lord. Four years after that bassist Reginald "Fieldy" Arvizu publicly proclaimed his faith in Christ. The enemy of our soul is not flesh and blood but a spiritual being. The One who battles for us is more than able to achieve victory and He fights in His way and His timing.

Seek First to Understand

1.   Think of a particular *situation* your son or daughter is in right now. It could be failure in school, trouble with the law, sickness, financial trouble, or toxic relationships. Can you *really* trust God with the outcome? With the process and the timing?

2.   Find one Biblical example where God intervened for a fragile person and completely changed a situation they were in. Read the whole story. Here are a few I like:

Rahab – God sent His messengers right into the guest bedroom of this prostitute. She believed the promise made to her. God not only spared her life but that of her whole family. She is in the lineage of Jesus.   *Joshua 2: 1-3, 6:17-25, Matthew 1:5*

Gideon – An Angel of the Lord finds him hiding in fear. He sees himself as weak and inferior. But God sees him as a valiant warrior, and he becomes what he was created to be. He is listed in the *Hall of Faith* in Hebrews chapter 11.   *Judges 6:11-8:21*

Samaritan Woman – The shameful secrets of this "loose" woman were laid bare as she was fetching her daily water in isolation from the decent ladies of the village. Her encounter with the One who didn't judge her changed her life and the lives of everyone she knew.   *John 4*

God's Word

*Do not be afraid for I AM with you...I will bring your children from the east
and gather you from the west....bring my sons from afar
and gather my daughters from the ends of the earth.*
Isaiah 43:5-6

Prayer

Lord, I have nearly drowned in my tears and my fears. But I trust You with my child. I believe that You are able and willing to just show up in both of our lives and gather us into your loving arms. I don't know when or how it will happen, but I believe change is coming. I thank You for your sweet presence and for reminding me of your faithfulness to do the impossible. In the Name of Jesus. Amen.

CHAPTER THREE

A Weaned Child

Lord, my heart is not haughty nor my eyes lofty.
Neither do I concern myself with great matters
nor with things too profound for me
Surely I have calmed and quieted my soul
Like a weaned child with his mother,
like a weaned child is my soul within me
O Israel, hope in the Lord from this time forth and forever.

Psalm 131 contains only three simple verses which calm me when I'm in distress. God understands the heart of a mother.

After only five days of living with an active addict I quickly relapsed into my old controlling behaviors – checking on him, wanting to intervene, counting his prescription meds, hiding my Nyquil and my purse. Only God's ways will not perish in eternal fire and be forgotten. I simultaneously anticipated getting him out of my house in a few days and dreaded the long separation during his treatment. Our minds and emotions are so untrustworthy. Only the Lord has a thorough overview of our whole situation and watches us as we struggle. He knows we don't need to.

A few days ago I was in my car, thinking again that after I saw my son through his addiction, <u>then</u> I would get focused on *kingdom work*, preaching the Word and ministering to other women. God's Spirit spoke to mine...*This IS your journey....*it doesn't begin after some event passes. *How* I get through these hard days is *how* I become more Christ-like. I'm trying to rush past what God is trying to use to change me, strengthen me, enable me.

The art of being still. *But I have stilled and quieted my soul; like a weaned child with its mother.* A nursing infant thrashes around screaming with anxiety as the hunger pangs strike, refusing to be quieted until the breast is in his mouth and his immediate need is met. A weaned child is content just to be with mom, knowing she is his trustworthy source of care. He wakes up each day thinking only about today – trusting that she will feed him, clean him, bandage a wound, and love him.

The weaned child has to still his own soul – this is an active act of the will to behave with the ever-increasing maturity of a growing child. Lord, this addiction is not only about my son, but importantly it is about me – my willingness to stop thrashing about demanding that You fix him so I can be happy. Rather I can be happy in Your Presence, waiting with a quiet soul while you arise to prepare my food at the proper time. You never forget that I need to eat, but you know when the time has come, what is available to me, and how it will nourish me precisely as I need.

Lord, my heart is not haughty...if it is, then I'm focusing on myself and my needs and my self-approval. Perhaps I am looking down from my pedestal with disapproval toward my child or another person that I am blaming for causing my anxiety.

Neither do I concern myself with great matters...how much time do I spend wondering exactly how God is going to work in my child's life, and when He is going to enable a breakthrough? I fret about the path my child will take. What will he do, when will he do it...only God knows and I cannot know. I must trust God's way. His timing is perfect.

nor with things too profound for me...why does my child not see what we see? Why does he not discern spiritual things? What is in his mind, his heart? God alone sees the heart of man. It is not mine to know.

I must *decide* to sit quietly with God and not be fretful, choosing a different behavior than I have learned or lived in the past. Contentment is in the spiritual woman. The Lord wants me to trust Him today for today's needs. He wants me to just love Him, be in relationship with him, and enjoy His protective presence. As a mother looks upon her growing child, so God looks upon me...loving me and watching me develop. He protects me from running out into the street, yet also lets me burn my hand on the stove so that I can learn not to do that again.

"O Israel, hope in the Lord from this time forth and forever"...my hope – the answers to my desires and dreams – all come from God – not people nor circumstances but from the Lord.

Seek First to Understand

1. What anxiety did you wake up with this morning?

2. What issue in your son's or daughter's life are you most concerned about right now?

3. If you think about this for the next 18 hours, what will change in his life?

4. Can you name one blessing in your life today? Three? Five?

5. Thank God for your son or daughter today and include one specific way they have blessed your life.

God's Word

Peace I leave with you; My (own) peace I now give and bequeath to you. Not as the world gives do I give to you. Do not let your hearts be troubled, neither let them be afraid. (Stop allowing yourselves to be agitated and disturbed; and do not permit yourselves to be fearful and intimidated and cowardly and unsettled.)
John 14:27 Amplified

Prayer

God, please forgive me for allowing anxiety to steal my peace. My worry has never changed anything. You have always fed me, given me shelter, and come to me as soon as I cried out for you. That will not change because You don't change. Let me see the good in this day. Help me enjoy my son as he is today. Help me enjoy Your Son as He is today and always. Thank you for teaching me to be still. In the Name of Jesus. Amen.

CHAPTER FOUR

Falling Off the Treadmill

I ponder another relapse into depravity I cannot comprehend. Lying and stealing not from strangers but from family. A shadowy life surrounded by other liars who use people like they use drugs. *Parties* where there is no laughter but dark rooms of death. Violence coming too close to home, with the windows of his car busted out in my quiet subdivision driveway last night while we slept, a warning to him. A room where poisonous needles are injected and Russian Roulette is played by the children of naïve but sleepless mothers. How could he do this again? To steal the baby's birthday money? To steal prescription medicines from a sick person who could not afford to replace them? To steal his brother-in-law's leather jacket to sell for a few dollars...this same brother-in-law he loves much more than he loves himself? This brother-in-law who has trusted him, counseled him, prayed for him?

I turn to the Word for some understanding of this.

For I do not understand my own actions (I am baffled, bewildered).
I do not practice or accomplish what I wish,
but I do the very thing that I loathe (which my moral instinct condemns).
Romans 7:15 Amplified

Paul, who wrote most of the New Testament, understood our human struggle.

Injection of a slowly lethal substance was not what I used to make the pain in my own hurt go away for a little while. But when I allow myself to remember my own sins and the confusion that was my life so many years ago, then it is easier to understand my son.

My weakness was always men. A victim of childhood sexual abuse, I was the Samaritan woman…leaving a trail of men. At least she wasn't married, but I was. I stole attention from my husband and my young children and gave it to someone else – a person totally unworthy of that adoration. I was a habitual liar – practiced at it. I wore lying like a garment, desperately trying to cover up sin. I was on a treadmill of destruction, and though I stepped off for a short time I always climbed back on when my need for escape was greater than my fear of getting caught and I needed something to make me feel good again.

I would rather not remember. It is not who I am today. I have a better life now. I recall it only because it helps me understand him. My drug of choice was different than his, but still I repeatedly did what I did not want to do, and my path was just as destructive.

Oh, but for the grace and mercy of God where would I be? Shall I credit myself with having dug myself out of the pit of hell and wonder why this foolish son of mine does not follow my righteous lead? No. It was God's mercy and compassion that caused me to finally get tired of my sin before my life was forever ruined.

So then God's gift is not a question of human will and human effort but of God's mercy. It depends not on one's own willingness nor on his strenuous exercise as in running a race, but on having God's mercy on him.
Romans 9:16 Amplified

May I never forget the extent of my own sins and even the ones I have not chosen to be finished with today.

There is therefore now no condemnation for those who are in Christ Jesus
Romans 8:1

This was my life-giving verse – the one that kept me going when the consequences of my own sinful nature slapped me in the face again.

In God's mercy he made the consequence of sin so painful that I had to get off that treadmill to nowhere and I fell into His waiting arms.

Grace was given to me – a gift. God knew there was someone worth redeeming on the treadmill of pain – going around and around again and again. He turned up the speed and elevated the pitch so I couldn't keep up. My heart was going to burst if I continued. Oh, thank you, God, for turning up the speed on my son's treadmill. He didn't want to be on the treadmill, but You looked at him and saw the pain that made him climb up there the first time. You saw what my mother-heart saw…the 9 year old boy full of laughter and fun and sensitivity, now a 20 year old buried in personal rejection, sin, and shame.

My gracious Father, let me remember today how far you have brought me so that I can release my son from the sting of my own accusations toward him.

If I could forgive him just a fraction of what You have forgiven me, then perhaps the wounds he will sustain when he falls will heal more quickly. Lord, your love and mercy toward me is undeserved and I am so very thankful for the blood of Jesus that washes away my sins every day.

Seek First to Understand

1. Be honest about the pain or embarrassment your child's addictive behaviors have caused you. When he lied to you, stole from you, was abusive to you, any, all, or more of these things, what did you feel?

   Anger
   Embarrassment
   Shame
   Fear

2. Think about what your own life was like before Jesus took over.

3. Are you afraid to forgive your child? What if you forgive him this time and he does it again. Can you trust God to deal with his sin problem just as he dealt with yours?

God's Word

If I forgive people their trespasses (their reckless and willful sins, leaving them, letting them go, and giving up resentment), my heavenly Father will also forgive me.
Matthew 6:14 Amplified

My Prayer

God of Mercy, I thank you with all that I am for saving me, for forgiving me and giving me another chance to get it right. I have allowed my own shame over my child's choices to keep me from forgiving him for what he has done. Because You have forgiven me, I choose to forgive my child for what he has done. I release him to you, knowing that only You know his pathway to healing. In the Name of Jesus. Amen

CHAPTER FIVE

Quiet my Tongue

*It is the glory of kings to search out a matter; it
is the glory of God to conceal a matter.*
Proverbs 25:2

How many times is God going to have to tell me this before I get it and change my behavior? I just joined a women's fitness center where there is a circle of machines, each designed to exercise one particular muscle group. When you have used all of them twice then you can focus on one or two machines where you know you need more work. This matter of my tongue is that message from God that I need to revisit because it still needs work.

I spent many years stuffing my feelings and hiding the secret of addictions in my family, first with my father and then my ex-husband, and the poison of resentment made me physically ill. In God's perfect timing,

I went through a 12-step program for codependency. There, over a period of nine months, I dug up the dead bones buried in my yard. During that season God enabled me to deal first with myself and then with others about the ways they had wounded me and I had wounded them. When I felt the release of getting the poisonous secrets out I vowed never again to stuff my feelings.

But now, with my son following in his father's footsteps in substance abuse, I had erred on the other side. Beginning with the first discovery of marijuana, I had alerted the parents of all his friends thinking, as heroines do, that I was doing them a good service and *not* thinking about the impact this would have on my relationship with my son. For several years with each traumatic event I kept the telephone lines sizzling as I recalled every fear, every wrong deed, every hurt he ever caused me with an assortment of friends and family. The result? He was embarrassed to come to church because he knew that everyone there knew his failures. He avoided family gatherings because he knew they knew all his sins and he felt condemned. He could not come to me with honesty because the *whole world* would know about it. And he was right.

I thought I had made progress. I had dealt with the past, but it had not fully translated into changed behavior to deal with new issues. I was learning to share less detail, and to protect his privacy while he healed. However, minus the details I was still telling new acquaintances that my son was in recovery for addiction and proudly announcing that he was X number of months clean and sober. Recently an older woman in my church reproved me, and told me not to speak of it, not to even see him in recovery but to see him healed and speak of him healed. I thought that seemed extreme and not balanced.

As I pondered this and examined my heart, as the Lord tells us to do, my spirit showed me that perhaps I was still enjoying a little martyrdom, the ever-patient mother. Two steps forward, one step back. It's still *all about me* isn't it, Lord? In my pondering and wandering through the Word, I came across this passage that spoke to the heart of this matter:

Had I spoken thus (and given expression to my feelings), I would have been untrue and have dealt treacherously against the generation of Your children. But when I considered how to understand this, it was too great an effort for me and too painful. Until I went into the sanctuary of God; then I understood...
Psalm 73:15-17 Amplified

My rehearsal of his sins only served to reinforce how I was seeing him today, not as I believed he could be and would be.

I will always need to deal with painful situations past or present. It is a mistake to bury the pain. Several times I have needed a professional counselor. Other times I needed to seek a trusted friend and talk about a particular issue because I could not sort out my thoughts. But most of the time all I really needed is to take it to my truest Friend, the one who searches my heart and my soul (mind, will, and emotions) and lets me see through His eyes.

The family members and intercessors who need to know where my son is physically located already know. It is important to my son not to add to his baggage by sending out news alerts of his struggles but rather to make his journey easier by giving the good report of the Lord.

Rehearsing the current status rehearses my fears. Speaking the truth of God's faithfulness to heal and restore releases my faith in the Healer. This is a challenging new behavior for me. My son is being challenged to take on a lot of new behaviors on his healing journey, and God is taking me to a new level of right *actions* as well. Thank you, Jesus.

He who began a good work in me will continue to complete it until Jesus comes back.
Philippians 1:6

I am such a work in progress!

Seek First to Understand

1. With how many people have you openly shared your child's recent failures?

2. Why did you share those things?

3. Has this indiscretion solved any problems or created more?

4. Do you have a lot of bones buried in your yard? What appropriate actions have you taken to deal with those?

God's Word

*May the words of my mouth and the meditation of my heart be pleasing in your sight,
O Lord, my Rock and my Redeemer*
Psalm 19:14 NIV

Help me, Lord, to keep my mouth shut and my lips sealed.
Psalm 141:3 TLB

A soft answer turns away wrath, but grievous words stir up anger.
Proverbs 15:1

The power of life and death are in the tongue. Now choose life.
Proverbs 18:21

Prayer

Lord, because you loved me you kept my dark secrets between You and I when I was wandering, revealing them in Your timing and Your way so that I could get help. You have trusted me to know some of my child's hidden ways. Please help me to follow your example, not adding to his hurt by opening my mouth to share ugly details.

Help me to come first to You, being honest about my pain, but trusting You to work in my child's life just like you worked in mine. I choose to speak life and not death about my child. In Jesus. Amen

THE LION, THE WITCH, AND THE WARDROBE
C. S. Lewis

"Oh, yes! Tell us about Aslan!" said several voices at once; for once again that strange feeling--like the first signs of spring, like good news, had come over them.

"Who is Aslan?" asked Susan.

"Aslan?" said Mr. Beaver. "Why, don't you know? He's the King. He's the Lord of the whole wood, but not often here, you understand. Never in my time or my father's time. But the word has reached us that he has come back. He is in Narnia at this moment. He'll settle the White Queen all right. It is he, not you, that will save Mr. Tumnus."

"She won't turn him into stone too?" said Edmund.

"Lord love you, Son of Adam, what a simple thing to say!" answered Mr. Beaver with a great laugh. "Turn him into stone? If she can stand on her two feet and look him in the face it'll be the most she can do and more than I expect of her. No, no. He'll put all to rights as it says in an old rhyme in these parts:

> Wrong will be right, when Aslan comes in sight,
> At the sound of his roar, sorrows will be no more,
> When he bares his teeth, winter meets its death,
> And when he shakes his mane, we shall have spring again."

CHAPTER SIX

Divine Warfare

They overcame him by the blood of the lamb and by the Word of their testimony.
Revelation 12:11

I was on a business trip in a hotel room in Cincinnati, Ohio. My three children were home alone. Their dad had moved out a few months earlier. I was always anxious when I had to leave them, though the girls were nearly through high school and very responsible. I remember it like it was yesterday.

I woke in the middle of the night. I was terrified. I saw a vision of my nine-year-old son in his bed. Hovering over him was a large black creature. I knew in my spirit it was Satan or a demonic force. I was too frightened to move. In fact, I felt pinned to my bed, my shoulders pressed against the mattress. My heart was pounding. Am I dreaming? I don't think so. I manage a whisper, "In the name of Jesus Christ, I command you to leave my son alone." Once I squeaked it out in a barely audible whisper, my voice got stronger. I said it over and over, louder and louder. I could breathe again. Sleep came. The next morning I remembered it again and thought myself a little crazy. Was it a dream? It didn't feel like a dream. I was sure I had been awake.

Over dinner that night, safely back home, I quietly posed the question. "Josh, did you have a bad dream last night?" His eyes got big. "How did you know?" he said. "Tell me what happened," I questioned, pretending it was no big thing. He said "I woke up and there was a monster in my room. I was scared. I put the covers over my head, and after a while he left."

Oh, Lord. I have not gone mad. God enabled me to protect my son from 600 miles away. Satan desired to destroy my son, but my boy had made a profession of faith in Christ at the age of 8. He belonged to Jesus, and Satan would not be allowed to kill him. Remembering this unique night years later, I trust the same God. Imprisoned in his drug use, he almost lost his life multiple times, yet God protected him.

The wonder of that night. Why would an evil force visit a child's room unless He feared a divine plan to use this life? God's arm of protection is so mighty. Why do I ever allow myself to get into fear and worry? Do I not yet understand that God's got him? It is not flesh and blood we fight against, but the spiritual forces of darkness. We fight in prayer. We war with the Word of God. Satan came to steal, kill, and destroy, but Jesus came that Josh would have life and have it to the full. God has watched over him and protected him and allowed me to know things so that I could take action, know *when* to pray, know *what* to pray, and know *how* to pray.

How many times did my mother intercede for me when she could see that I was not thinking straight or acting like I had an ounce of sense? Oh, Lord, you are faithful to protect us. You discipline us because you love us, but you have not allowed the enemy to kill us because we are Yours and we have not completed our purpose.

He knows my getting up and my lying down. He knew me when I was in my mother's womb. He called my name. He put in my mother's head what I should be called. He put in my head what my son should be called. My name and my son's name mean *Grace*. How much we have needed it.

When we seek the face of God in our desperation, we learn to recognize the Holy Spirit's voice. We know that we need to pray even when we don't know the details. We obey. We fight this battle and that battle. Then we rest from a battle, having done our part for the moment. We never lay our armor down, but we can put it at our side for the moment. The Commander can see the entire battlefield. He has the combat plan. He calls forward the troops – his intercessors – when they are needed.

Seek First to Understand

Remember a time when God intervened in such a way that you knew without a doubt it was Him. Write it down and save the paper. You will need to refer to it in the future to encourage yourself in the Lord.

God's Word

*I have given you authority to trample on snakes and scorpions
and to overcome all the power of the enemy.*
Luke 10:19

Prayer

Father, thank you for giving me the weapons I need to do battle for my child's life. You are in charge of this war. I yield myself to your commands. Help me to hear Your voice or remember Your words at critical moments in my child's life. Thank you for the peace you give me when I do the small part you ask of me. In the Name of Jesus. Amen

CHAPTER SEVEN

Remembering the Good

Between ages 18 and 19 the tattoos appeared. The first one was the head of Christ on his left shoulder. Then on his right forearm appeared a cross on its side, with *Philppians 4:13* written next to it. The tattoo artist likely had no idea who the Philippians were nor that he had dropped an *i*. I was not upset at the early tattoos because I *chose* to see the hand of God in it, making excuses for what I could not control.

Years earlier I had marked *Isaiah 44:2-5* in my Bible and written the names of my three children by those promises about the offspring of believers: Josh's name was written by ...*still another will write on his hand 'the Lord's' and will take the name Israel.* In my meditations God showed me that our vocation is executed with our hands, and from that time on I believed that my son would someday work for God. When the two tattoos on his arms were Christian symbols, I received it as confirmation that God would put him on the right track.

But in dealing with addiction, there are two steps forward and one step back. A skull with a rose in its mouth soon appeared on the other shoulder. Then a cityscape across his back. Then miscellaneous swirls which surrounded the Philippians scripture reference so that it no longer stood out. When our children are running from God, there are many more bleak days than inspiring ones. On those many days when disappointment face-slapped me with another relapse, arrest, or *bad news call*...I had to will myself to remember the good.

Finally my brothers, whatever is true, whatever is noble, whatever is right, whatever is pure, whatever is lovely, whatever is admirable—
if anything is excellent or praiseworthy—think about such things.
Philippians 4: 8

Do this and peace follows.

In order for me to extend grace to my child, I had to deliberately see the good in him and not only the pain inflicted on the family by his behavior. What is there about him that is good? I made a list:

✓ He has a great sense of humor and a quick wit – he has made me laugh out loud countless times and that has been good for my soul.
✓ When he was seven or eight and his father had recently left us, he spent $89, every penny he had saved up, to buy me a boombox for Mother's Day. It was a supremely unselfish act of love and I needed that.
✓ He loves babies, animals, and old people. There's something intrinsically good in his nature.

✓ He is a loyal friend, and while that has also been his downfall — protecting his drug-using running buddies — the characteristic of loyalty in itself is good. God can use that.
✓ He is very affectionate, often running his hands through my hair and sitting on the sofa with one arm swung around my neck.
✓ He loves family time.
✓ He genuinely cares about the spiritual condition of his fellow prisoners.

While I must deal with the truth of his addiction and the evil that comes with it, I must also remember the good and speak it out of my mouth at appropriate times. The truth is, my son is who God says he is, not what others say. He is not what I see with my natural eyes nor what my own mind conjures up.

On those many days when doubt wants to close in on me, I rehearse God's word concerning sons of the faith.

Sons are a heritage from the Lord...like arrows in the hands of a warrior...
I will not be put to shame.
Psalm 127:3-5

And

Your sons will be like olive shoots around your table.
Psalm 128:3

God has given me this child. He didn't give him to any other mother. He is God's gift to me. And God will continue to perfect us both.

Seek First to Understand

1. Choose to remember the good.

2. What qualities do you remember in your child when he was 5? 10?

3. What is it about him that makes you smile?

4. Look back through his baby book, artwork, or old cards you have kept to help you remember the child that God created.

5. Write down five good qualities you remember about your child, even if they aren't showing themselves right now.

God's Word

For you created my inmost being; you knit me together in my mother's womb.
I praise you because I am fearfully and wonderfully made;
your works are wonderful; I know that full well.
Psalm 139: 13-14

Prayer

Loving Father, my child is a blessing from You. A child given by You provides something of great value to the family, and I thank You for this gift that You gave us. You make no mistakes. What You make is good. Thank you that I am not ashamed of my child. Refresh my happy memories and give me a grateful heart as I meditate on what is good about him. In the Name of Jesus. Amen.

CHAPTER EIGHT

A Pile of Rocks

Go over before the Ark of the Lord your God into the middle of the Jordan.
Each of you is to take up a stone upon his shoulder. In the future when your
descendants ask their fathers, 'What do these stones mean?'
tell them 'Israel crossed the Jordan on dry ground.'
For the Lord your God dried up the Jordan before you until you had crossed over.
Joshua 4:5-6, 21-24

Why did God want a pile of stones set on the riverbank of the Jordan? So the Israelites would see the stones that came from the middle of a river at flood stage and remember that God had done a miracle for them as they crossed over on dry ground where those stones had been.

Looking back at the pages of my journals I review the pile of stones. They would be insignificant grey rocks to those unable to see what I see.

Rock #1. At eight years of age, Josh announced he wanted to be water baptized. His dad opposed it and refused to come, suggesting that he was being brainwashed. But this child was adamant that he would not be denied what was his, and the ceremony of dedication to God took place on a Sunday morning at a Baptist Church in Wentzville, Missouri.

Rock #2. Three years later, he stood up on the platform at our small church, having just returned from a youth retreat, and announced that God had called him to the mission field. It was his particular words that still ring in my mind. He said he had seen a vision of a black child with a large stomach, and God had told him he would see things he did not want to see.

Rock #3. We had a small high school graduation party for him. He was in the gifted student program as an elementary student. Twelve years later, he had graduated from a *special* high school designed for kids who weren't going to make it through a regular high school program. We weren't in a position to celebrate his academic achievements. I knew this gathering needed to be uniquely spiritual, and it was. People who loved him gathered. After the customary food, the believers took turns talking about his good qualities....leadership, humor, charisma. A gathering of male relatives and friends encircled him and laid hands on him and prayed for him to walk with God for a blessed life.

Rock #4. In his first 28-day rehabilitation program, he stood on the platform to tell about himself. He said that his church training had given him his spiritual foundation. No phony elaboration, but it had made the list of the ten formative events in his life.

Rock #5. When we moved him to Tulsa in the first relocation for sobriety, he joined three church Bible studies and volunteered with the youth group. He was reaching out for God's life in the only way he knew how. During that year, God brought five strong believing men into his life. Each spoke to him about his relationship with Jesus, encouraged him, and prayed for him.

Rock #6. In the long-term treatment facility where he would take his stand for sobriety, he shared with me that he had had an *epiphany*. He had awakened one night with a realization that he had denied the Presence of God because he didn't want to stop doing what he was doing. But suddenly he knew God was real. It was such important knowledge to him that he got up out of bed and wrote it down.

Rock #7. Six months into his long-term treatment, Josh was allowed to start working in the community under close watch. He called one day to tell me that something had happened and he didn't know what to think of it. He had been working at the coffee shop when his co-worker just disappeared. She didn't tell anyone she needed a break, but she suddenly wasn't on the job. When the customers stopped coming in he went looking for her and found her outside leaning up against the wall. She was a thirty-something woman, married, and he believed she was a Christian. They knew almost nothing about each other. He had never shared with her that he was in a treatment program, and it was deliberately kept confidential by the managers of the popular coffee store. She told him that she was working inside and felt like the Holy Spirit was speaking to her about him and she was to write it down. No pen to write with, she grabbed a napkin and a marker and took it outside. This is exactly what was written on the napkin: *"God is raising you up as a powerful. You will be instrumental in bring multitudes into his kingdom. He is so pleased with you. He wants you to know that he is with you. Knows the areas you are weak and will be your strength as you look to him. You are going to be used mightily. Promotion is coming to you. He is advancing you because he knows your heart. Don't look to your circumstances and think your not able. He is opening up doors for you. Trust in him and believe he loves you and has plans to prosper you. You may have to overcome some obstacles but you will triumph and it is to strengthen you for the days ahead. You are an evangelist and are effective. People respect trust and admire you. It is my Favor that is with you."* God spoke to him through a stranger, encouraging him in a way that only He can.

My son's walk with God is his alone. Each of us is given self-will and opportunity to accept or reject. Just as Jesus' mother Mary pondered in her heart the things that were being said about her son, I remembered and recorded the spiritual milestones. Each grey rock helped me on bleak days to know that God is building a monument to Himself. He has always been there as the architect, the builder, stone upon stone. Ultimately my son will look back at what seemed like heavy boulders in his arms at the time, and he will see that he was building a tribute to God's faithfulness.

Perhaps neither you nor your child have ever had anyone speak over you on behalf of the Lord. Do not be discouraged. We hear from God in different ways. People I know and trust have heard an audible voice. I have not. Some write music or poetry given to them by God. I do not. For me, at times when I'm reading my Bible a verse will just jump out at me. I meditate on that verse and I see what it means for my own life. Other times I am just living my daily life when suddenly an idea will pop into my head...an understanding of a situation or what action to take. I believe those are God-moments. He is throwing me a life raft. My most memorable times of prayer happen when I am outdoors in the woods or by water. I feel His presence and I may cry, but then I am at peace. He is with me and He's going to help me. You will learn to listen carefully to words spoken to you by people whom you believe know the Lord. He *speaks* or reveals Himself to everyone who seeks. Think deeply about these next questions.

Seek First to Understand

1. As a young innocent, did your child ever express any belief or thanksgiving to God?

2. Can you recall any spiritual milestones in your son's life? Baptism? Vacation Bible School? Catechism classes? First Holy Communion? Youth group or retreat? At what age did they occur?

3. Did God send spiritual leaders into his life? What did they do?

4. Write these things down. No matter how small it may have seemed at the time, write.

5. If you do not already journal, begin now to record what you see God doing. Resist the urge to over-analyze the outcome of each stone, but make a note of what you recall.

6. Begin to add scriptures that speak about children, sons, descendants, heirs. Read the whole context. Meditate on those scriptures.

God's Word

Yet this I call to mind and therefore I have hope.
Because of the Lord's great love we are not consumed, for his compassions never fail.
They are new every morning; great is your faithfulness.
I say to myself, "The Lord is my portion; therefore I will wait for him.
Lamentations 3:21-24

Prayer

Father, You have proven yourself over and over. Just as You brought me through my old life, You will cause my child to cross through the dangerous flood waters on dry ground. Thank You for all the times You showed me in Your wonderful word that I could count on You. Thank You for keeping Your hand on my child and letting him feel Your presence. Thank You that he will be able to look back and see that You never left his side, and he will praise You. In Jesus. Amen.

CHAPTER NINE

Not Lost but Found

few weeks before my son entered his first 28 day program, he and I visited a church together. I had often talked to him about the importance of giving to church but it was never a priority to him. On this particular day he slipped a $10 bill into the offering plate, nudging me so I would notice. He made it a point to tell me about it again in the car. I assured him that God would return it to him.

Then the nightmare began with my discovery of drug paraphernalia in my home and his confession of heroin addiction. After a hospital stay for detoxification, he was moved to a treatment facility in Boonville, Missouri. I went to visit him after the first week. Conversation was limited between us. To kill some time we took a drive to the only scenic spot in the area, a scraggly little town park. Within that park, a small windy road leads to the top of a bluff overlooking the Missouri River. I parked the car and walked over to the edge to admire the view and take a deep breath and try to concentrate on something other than my son and our inability to talk to each other. Josh didn't walk over with me. I noticed him pick up a piece of paper off the ground near my car. He walked over and said it was a winning lottery ticket that had not been redeemed. Not a fan of the lottery, I was skeptical. But I drove him to a nearby grocery store and sure enough, it was good for $15, fifty percent more than he had placed in the offering plate.

I was touched that God found him at the top of a cliff in the middle of nowhere to keep His word and to let him know that he was not lost. God knew right where he was and He had his eye on him. Psalm 139:7 says, *I can never escape from your Spirit! I can never get away from your Presence.*

No matter where my son wanders off to, God watches over him. And God knew right where I was. He knew I didn't know how to talk to my son. I was frightened. I was mistrustful. I was doubtful, confused, and embarrassed.

Immediately I sensed when I went to the Valley Hope Center that there was an atmosphere of acceptance. Each of the residents seemed to genuinely like the other patients, understand them, and care about them. I was acutely aware of the discomfort of the visiting family members. We avoided eye contact with each other. We stood around with our purses clutched tight or hands in our pockets. We surveyed the scene of the walking dead, all smoking, most unkempt, dress tees with skulls on them, all ages, shapes, sizes, and races in various stages of detoxification. I wondered how any of us got to this place and whether we would ever again be *normal.*

I sensed that my son felt okay here. He felt not judged, probably for the first time in many years that he could remember. After a four-day stay a few weeks later I made some marginal steps toward loving my son and others there, even knowing that many of them would fall again. Surrounded with broken lives, my compassion was stirred toward the others there who had lost husbands and wives, children, jobs, all self-respect, and freedom. This is easier to do for those who don't touch your own life, but much more difficult when that person is causing an enormous disruption in *normal* in your own life.

There exists a nasty judgmental spirit that so quickly rises up from my heart into my eyes and betrays me, even when I manage to control my tongue. As I wrote down scriptures to commit to memory, these eventually got into my spirit.

Do not judge or you too will be judged. For in the same way you judge others you will be judged and with the measure you use it will be measured to you.
Matthew 7:1

And:

Who are you to judge someone else's servant? To his own master he stands or falls.
And he will stand, for the Lord is able to make him stand.
Romans 14:4

Truth is in God's word. It divides soul and spirit. It cuts through the pretense of who we would like to be into who we really are. God knew that in spite of my love for my son, my shame spun off into judgment and condemnation. He would make progress, but what about me? Could I change? Could I see both my son and his dad through my

61

Father's eyes? Could I ever learn to feel what the Heavenly Father feels when He looks at them?

He gave us few actual commands. The most important? Love Him and love others, because He loves them. The sins of my son and his fellow patients became more visible than mine, but I could so easily have stepped off into that same abyss. I was spared this public humiliation but God knew my many sins. Can I love him enough to let him bear the consequences so that his choices hurt and he will crave change? Can I love him enough to do it without rebuke in my voice or vengeance in my actions? The Spirit of God weeps over us all when we sin.

Seek First to Understand

1. How does God find you today? Angry? Depressed? Self-righteous?

2. Have you judged anyone today? A stranger's appearance or their actions in public? A celebrity in the news? A parent? Your husband? Your child?

3. Have you ever felt judged by anyone? How did it make you feel?

4. Was that person in the church or a professed believer? Did that especially hurt?

5. How would you feel today if *that* secret sin of yours was in an email message or a Facebook post being shared out of *concern* for you?

6. Sing the first verse of Amazing Grace and listen with your heart.

    Amazing Grace, how sweet the sound
    That saved a wretch like me
    I once was lost but now am found
    Was blind but now I see

God's Word

I praise you because I am fearfully and wonderfully made; your works are wonderful.
Psalm 139:14

Above all, love each other deeply, because love covers over a multitude of sins.
I Peter 4:8

Let your conversation always be full of grace.
Colossians 4:6

Prayer

Merciful God, thank You that I am not lost to You. You know right where I am and everything I feel today. Your own Son did not judge. I ask Your forgiveness for judging Your servants, including my child, his dad, his friends, and his drug dealers. It is only before You that my child will stand or fall. Thank You that You <u>are able</u> to make him stand and You <u>will</u> make him stand. In the Name of Jesus. Amen.

CHAPTER TEN

Speak the Word

I believe, therefore I speak.
2 Corinthians 4:13

I was in Sunday School as a child, then I walked away from God at 18 when my mother died and my faith died with her. When I finally crawled back to Jesus at the age of 32, I spent twenty years in a variety of churches. We sat quietly singing the hymns and listening as the pastor or another leader prayed for this sick person and that sick person, but nothing seemed to really change in my life. When there was chaos in my alcoholic home, I could be found in my rocking chair with my Bible, or out on the porch swing with my Bible, quietly seeking peace. The marriage ended, and I survived, and there was a measure of peace because the daily angry words and accusations and profanity had stopped for a season. But I knew there was more. I knew I was supposed to be able to walk in victory over my circumstances.

In the midst of the crisis with my son, God began to help me understand that I couldn't just rock my way to victory; that had not saved my marriage and it would not save my son. I had to fight for my son's life. The words had to come out of my mouth before they could get in my soul.

Bless (affectionately, gratefully praise) the Lord, you His angels, you mighty ones who
do His commandments, hearkening to the voice of His word.
Psalm 103:20 Amplified

God spoke the world into existence. *And God said…* Genesis 1:3. In all my years in one church and another, no one had ever shown me this or demonstrated it. The spoken Word has power.

The Holy Spirit revealed this to me, and then my ears were opened to others whom God was using to reinforce this truth of the power of the spoken word. Joyce Meyer's life had been transformed when she realized this truth, and she was teaching it. I had never received it as God's truth until I began to apply it to my battle for my son's life.

A decade later I heard Dr. Caroline Leaf teach about changing our lives by speaking God's truth and not Satan's lies out of our mouths. I absorbed all of her books. Every memory is created by a thought and has a corresponding emotion stored with it. Most of our thoughts come from input from one of our five senses. What we see, taste, smell, touch, and hear forms a thought and gets stored in our cerebral cortex as a memory. Those memories are stored on a neuron which looks a lot like a tree. We add branches to the tree with each experience. An emotion is also stored in a little almond-shaped organ called the *amagdala*. When our experience is a bad one, the brain releases chemicals which race through our body and also flood that section of the brain where we stored that memory. Dr. Leaf calls them *toxic thoughts*. When we have enough of those toxic thoughts our brain is filled with something resembling a dark cloud. She calls it fear. When another similar experience happens and more branches are formed on that same tree, it becomes the attitude of our mind or the way we think. We are filled with fear. Our gut reaction to another similar bad experience is to react the way we always react because our emotions go into default mode of fear, anger, or depression.

The good news is we can literally change our brains and those knee-jerk reactions. The way to change the attitude of our minds is to believe what God says about me and those I'm fighting for. When I believe it and speak it, those words out of my own mouth are coming right back into my ears as new input to create another better thought. Enough of those and the black cloud goes away and our body is lopping off those bad tree branches and putting new healthy ones in their place. In John's gospel Jesus said:

I am the true grapevine, and my father is the gardener. He cuts off every branch of mine that doesn't produce fruit, and he prunes the branches that do bear fruit so they will produce even more. You have already been pruned and purified by the message I have given you. Remain in me, and I will remain in you. For a branch cannot produce fruit if it is severed from the vine, and you cannot be fruitful unless you remain in me.
John 15:1-4

He explained it to us and in our time we are blessed by science to understand how our brain works.

The Lord began to train me to use the weapon He had given me. As I read and prayed, I would suddenly be drawn to a certain scripture and I would understand it in a way that before I had not. I looked up words in the concordance. I absorbed any scripture having to do with children or with sons in particular. If my heart leapt when I read, then I took that as my own word from God, and I wrote it out on an index card. Before long I had about 50 cards with a scripture on both sides. I began to take walks in the park with my cards, speaking them out loud as I walked. I took them on airplanes. I carried them in my purse. I took them to Romania and Moldova on a mission trip. They went where I went. They began to seep into my memory so that I could say them whenever bad news about my son came and fear was seeping in. As I was speaking God's will then I could see from His perspective, and my fears began to disappear. The emotions I now felt were loving and strong.

When I was feeling ashamed of my child's failures or my own failures? *Behold, I will create a new heaven and a new earth. The former things will not be remembered, nor will they come to mind. Isaiah 65:17*

When his character appeared anything but Godly? *The law of his God is in his heart; his feet do not slip. Psalm 37:31* Believe it *for him* while he can't believe it for himself. See him as God sees him.

When I wondered about his future? *He who fears the Lord has a secure fortress, and for his children it will be a refuge. Proverbs 14:26* and *Their descendants will be known among the nations, and their offspring among the peoples. All who see them will acknowledge that they are a people the Lord has blessed. Isaiah 61:9*

When money slipped through his hands like water? *I was young and now am old, yet I have never seen the righteous forsaken or their children begging bread. Psalm 37:25*

68

When he had cursed me, hung up on me, or slammed doors so hard the house rattled? *The good man brings good things out of the good stored up in him for out of the overflow of the heart the mouth speaks.* *Luke 6:45*

When I can't remember not dealing with addiction and my brain is tired? *Yet this I call to mind and therefore have hope…because of the Lord's great love we are not consumed, for his compassions never fail, they are new every morning. Great is Your faithfulness.* *Lamentations 3:21-24* Some scriptures you will speak every day.

When I wanted to scream back at him or the kid next door who is selling him drugs? *Do not be overcome with evil but overcome evil with good.* *Romans 12:21*

When I'm feeling responsible for his life? *And all thy children shall be taught of the Lord; and great shall be the peace of thy children.* *Isaiah 54:13*

In the early ages of mankind there was no parchment and even God's words to Abraham and Moses were not written down. They were passed down verbally, word for word, and memorized by each generation. They were only written down by the Israelites about 600 years before Christ came to earth. They were being taken into captivity by the Babylonians and they didn't want to lose God's word. Think of the power of being able to recite entire books of His words. The Israelites went on to accomplish amazing things and still do to this day. They know who they are. We can begin to walk in power and not fear when we literally take God's words as truth about who we are and who our child is.

The next stage in changing the way I was thinking about my son was to personalize those scriptures on my index cards. I verbally put his name into the promises of God.

*Thank you Jesus that **Josh** is 'like an olive shoot around my table' fruit bearing, and productive. Psalm 128:3*

*Thank you God that **Josh** will be well-known, and that those who pity him now will be praising you as they see how you have blessed him. Isaiah 61:9*

*Thank you Lord that **Josh** is a good man who speaks good things because his heart is good before you. Luke 6:45*

*Praise You Jesus for Your faithfulness is new every morning and you will be faithful to heal **Josh** and deliver us both from our bondage. Lamentations 3:24*

*Thank you God for enabling **Josh** and me to treat others well and thus to overcome all the evil intentions of the enemy." Romans 12:21*

*Thank You Lord for your personal plan to teach **Josh** and the peaceful life you have in store for him. Isaiah 54:13*

Seek First to Understand

If you could replay what you said today about your child, how much of it expressed fear even if you didn't explicitly use the word fear?

God's Word

Meditate: *The tongue has the power of life and death and those who love it will eat its fruit. Proverbs 18:21*

Speak: *It is written, 'I believed, therefore I have spoken.' With that same spirit of faith, we also believe and therefore speak. 2 Corinthians 4:13*

Act: *Take the helmet of salvation and the sword of the Spirit, which is the word of God. Ephesians 6:17*

Prayer

Father, I praise You for the power of your spoken word. Thank You for showing me how to pray Your thoughts and Your will over myself and my child. It is Your will that my child live and not die before his full life. You gave me the authority to represent You in the earth, and I will speak for You. My words are life-giving. Set a guard over my tongue so that I am stopped when negative words or lies try to creep back out of my mouth. I will overcome the plan of Satan by the blood of the lamb and the word of my testimony. In the Name of Jesus.

CHAPTER ELEVEN

Across an Ocean

I knew Josh was in trouble with drugs again when it was time for me to leave the United States to lead women's conferences in Romania and Moldova. Five years earlier I would have cancelled every plan to stay home and be in charge of his crisis. I still had codependency issues and I had made a lot of progress but I didn't know how to heal myself. A bedrock scripture on my pathway to wholeness was:

> *He who began a good work in me will continue to perfect me*
> *until the day of Christ Jesus.*
> *Philippians 1:6.*

Oh, how I needed perfecting! This time I got on the plane.

We held the first conference in Iasi, Romania. I shared some things with the women about my son's battles with drugs and my battles with releasing him to God. I taught them how to speak the Word of God over their children. My testimony of faith would be greatly tested 24 hours later. The van was packed and we were preparing to leave Romania to head to Moldova later that day when I received the first email from my daughter, Andrea. I could tell that she was carefully choosing her words and sparing me many details. I could have spent the money for a long distance call but in truth I didn't want to. He was using again. Her husband, Jim, was banging on Josh's locked apartment door, knowing he was critically ill, and begging him to open the door so they could talk. I struggled with shame and fear.

We had relocated Josh to Oklahoma thinking magically that simply being in a different city would make him well. When he got released from the first residential rehabilitation center in Boonville, Missouri, they asked him what plan he had to stay clean. He said "move to Oklahoma," and I quickly agreed. On the day we left to drive him down there with U-Haul in tow, he was so high he couldn't drive. As if we didn't see it, we continued on. We enrolled him in community college, set him up in an apartment, and arranged a monthly deposit to him which would cover his living expenses. He was set up in an outpatient program in Tulsa with a small group of other people on drugs, but he skipped a lot of meetings. Even then I could not clearly see the insanity of giving an addict money and expecting him to use it for groceries, rent, and utilities. Jim and Andrea had been married less than a year. Andrea was a big sister extraordinaire. They were close, and she was like a second mother. She and Jim both loved Josh, and somehow we all thought that some one of us or all of us together could just love him enough to make him want to get well.

The next day another email arrived. Josh's dad was enroute from St. Louis to Tulsa. I had always been the one who took him to doctors, made calls, found rehab centers, worked with the insurance companies, and kept a vigil while he got through his treatment programs. Rarely will a rehab center take an active heroin addict unless they have been through detoxification at a hospital because they can get so sick in the process. James had committed to get him through detox and get him into a treatment program. I was grateful but also struggling because I wasn't *there for him.*

I sat in the office in Iasi, Romania, and I sobbed. I thanked God that He was continuing to watch over my son while I was 6,000 miles away doing what God had instructed me to do. He was showing me so clearly that I could not heal my son, but He could.

My messages for the women in Ungheni, Moldova, were carefully planned. I wanted to teach about prosperity. I did not want to talk about my son or myself, but only about what the Word says about financial provision to these desperately poor women. I was sure that was what they needed. There were four speakers and I was near the last. I was to speak on Saturday. Attendance at the Friday night session was good, but almost no one responded for prayer. No great move of God happened. Eastern European women tend to hold their emotions close. They don't share their dark secrets and those burdens show on their hardened faces. The women received the welcome gifts and the meal prepared for them, but they scurried for the door when the evening session was ended.

I was so troubled that night. Five of us were sharing the pastor's tiny apartment, and I was sharing a fold-out sofa with a woman I had just met. I could not sleep. At 3:30 a.m. I crept out of the living/bedroom we shared and felt my way in the dark to the kitchen, the only other available room. There was only a table, no chairs. I sat on the cold linoleum floor with my open Bible praying. *What's wrong, Lord?* In the quiet of that early morning, I felt the Holy Spirit nudge me to tell my story to these women. My son had just fallen again, and I didn't know his condition. Would the truth even be an encouragement to them? I didn't want to do it, but I obeyed.

It was my turn to speak; I began to tell them about growing up with sexual abuse and rage, then the heartbreak of losing my marriage due to alcoholism and adultery. I told them that my son was even now in a rehabilitation center fighting for his life and his soul. But I also told them that God had gotten me through the darkest days of my past and He would get me through these days and heal my son. Speaking from my heart, I shared that God cared about them so much that He had me stay here and complete the conference schedule rather than run home. There was a tremendous change in the atmosphere. These women didn't know that American women could understand them. But God knew that many women suffered with family addictions and problems with children that exceeded anything I had experienced. At the lunch break, they were standing in line for prayer. First was the wife of an alcoholic with suffering etched into her young face, flanked by her two teenage daughters. She prayed for salvation and made an appointment with the pastor. Heartbroken women lined up to share sorrowful stories of children who had gone to Ukraine to find work and never been heard from again. At the end of that night, each of us was surrounded by women hungry for prayer, for encouragement, for deliverance. The entire staff of a local children's orphanage received the Lord that night. The women were reluctant to leave. There were warm hugs exchanged. A bond of sisterhood was established even though we did not speak the same language. Giving my testimony and proclaiming that God would deliver my son built my confidence in *The Healer* as I spoke the words.

At that time no one had a laptop and there were no internet cafes in this town of 15,000 people. I had no email contact from Moldova so I didn't know what was happening in Tulsa. I was aware of it and yet not troubled by it. I felt strangely free of it. There was nothing I could do about it and my only option was to trust God. It was the *peace that passeth understanding.*

The next conference was in Chisinau, the capital city. The local team on the ground had not prepared to the satisfaction of our ministry leader and they were offended by him. There was confusion and disunity. In our preparation meetings and as we drove through the city, I noted that these women were not like the village women, who wore simple long skirts, practical shoes, headscarves, no makeup and no jewelry. The Chisinau women dressed like stylish Americans. In prayer I had to battle my fears that what I had to say was not relevant to them. The first night I did not speak. After 30 minutes of begging by the local pastor, three women came forward for salvation. The next night I would speak. But now I knew that the story of my struggle was what God would use to reach those whose hearts were hardened by life. That night I started immediately to talk about my healing from codependency at the end of a 30 year marriage. I talked about my son's addiction and praised God that He was in charge of Josh's healing while I was in another country serving Him. I added a contest that pitted two women in a race up the aisle against two other women. But one team had a leg tied together inside a feed sack. *You can't run your race if you have your leg in somebody else's bag.* They got it. That night many women received salvation and deliverance. There were testimonies of physical healings. There was great excitement in the house about God's mighty power.

But God wasn't finished with me. He wanted to show me His deep and abiding love. The pastor's wife had called the speakers up to the platform to thank us and give us a gift. Suddenly she called for the women to pray specifically for my son. Two hundred and fifty women began to pray out loud in Russian, Romanian, English, and their spiritual language. They prayed for my son's complete healing and restoration. They proclaimed it as fact and praised God for it. I felt the power of God wash over me like a warm wave. I wept uncontrollably but simultaneously breathed in the Presence of God. Three different women in attendance came to me when the conference ended and all three said they had heard from God and my son would live and be healed.

> *If I rise on the wings of the dawn, if I settle on the far side of the sea,*
> *even there your hand will guide me, your right hand will hold me fast.*
> *Psalm 139:9*

Ten days after I returned to the States I made my way down to Oklahoma and another visit to a rehabilitation center. I never stopped caring, but I was more removed from the process this time. I was beginning to let go. Three more months of agony followed. At the end of the program, it was determined that Josh would move into a *halfway house* with strict rules and living with other recovering addicts. I had to clean up his apartment and store the furniture. I had never been in a pawn shop, but I visited several of them in search of my television, Jim's leather jacket, a computer and other items he had pawned to get drug money. He only lasted two weeks in the halfway house before he was caught using and kicked out on the street. One of his few Tulsa friends died from an overdose complicated by Hepatitis C. Shortly after that we learned that Josh had been sharing needles with him; he had contracted the disease and his liver was damaged. Those were scary days. But strength came from remembering the words and the prayers spoken by 250 women 6,000 miles away, women whom I will not see again until Heaven.

> *I will contend with him that contendeth with thee,*
> *and I will save thy children.*
> Isaiah 49:25b

In the past ten years I have traveled over 150,000 miles to teach other women how to believe God's promises. Almost always, Josh works his way into my teaching and his story always has an impact. God will use our trials and testimonies to make a difference in other people's lives.

Seek First to Understand

1. What are you passionate about? That is usually a good indication of the natural and spiritual gift that God has given you for His purposes in your lifetime. Write down two or three things that you are really good at.

2. Has the Spirit of God been stirring up a desire to use that gift to help people? In one sentence describe what need you would like to meet among the unchurched or within the Body of Christ.

3. If you were totally free, what would you start doing to bring your passion to life?

God's Word

"For the Lord is the Spirit,
and wherever the Spirit of the Lord is, there is freedom."2 Corinthians 3:17

For you have been called to live in freedom, my brothers and sisters.
but don't use your freedom to satisfy your sinful nature.
Instead, use your freedom to serve one another in love.
Galatians 5:13

God has given each of you a gift from his great variety of spiritual gifts.
Use them well to serve one another.
I Peter 4:10

For God's gifts and his call can never be withdrawn.
Romans 11:29

Prayer

Father, thank you for the gifts you have given me. I know that you have not forgotten me. You planned for me at this unique time to make a Kingdom difference. I am not too late. My heart's desire is to serve you and help others that you have chosen for me. Thank you for what I have learned in the hard places I have walked with my child and how you will use it for your glory. I am willing, Lord. Help me to walk in freedom. In Jesus Name, Amen.

CHAPTER TWELVE

Praying for Life

If anyone sees his brother commit a sin that does not lead to death,
he should pray and God will give him life.
I John 5:16

My friend Darla drove with Josh and I down to Florida to take him to Haven House. She had lost her 18 year old son to drugs only 4 years earlier. She had a special love for my son. She told me that she considered that we were now *sharing* him. I felt no jealousy over this. I understood that she needed to have a part in seeing Josh live and not die. I could always talk to her about what was happening in Josh's life and not fear judgment. He felt the same and it created a comfortable atmosphere as we made the thirteen hour drive. We all need each other.

Four years earlier a small circle of women had been gathered at church for our weekly prayer meeting. Darla's son Nate had joined the

Marines and was scheduled to leave for boot camp the next morning. We prayed for him to have success in the military, believing it was his only chance for a normal life. But he never got on the bus to Marine camp. He and some friends decided instead to have one last party before they went off to their brave new futures. Someone, perhaps a relative, sneaked in the liquor. Indeed, it was Nate's last party and his last day of life. A lethal combination of drugs and alcohol caused him to drown in his own vomit. His young heart stopped beating.

Our agony was compounded by a crisis of faith. Was he already dead when we prayed? Did God not hear our prayers? We searched our memories and desperately tried to recall any sign of his true commitment to the Lord. We can take comfort in God's character. He is just and fair. Nate would have had his opportunity. We do not get to know everything this side of heaven. We would not be able to deal with all that knowledge. There are many reasons why prayers are hindered. At some point God says *enough,* and sin takes its consequences. We don't always know what is in another's heart. We do know that God gives us all free will, and we must first of all choose Him.

I searched for answers and struggled to keep my faith in God's Word. Jesus, help me to understand! I saw this truth in I John 5:16. A *brother* is one in the family of faith. This is always a term used to describe not bloodline but spiritual family. A sin that leads to death is blasphemy against the Holy Spirit – unbelief. It is the Spirit that draws us into saving faith. If I reject the Spirit of Truth, I have rejected the only source of my eternal life – Jesus Christ – and I cannot pray a person into heaven who has willfully rejected their Savior. Only God knows the condition of Nate's heart and what decision he made.

Out of his own mouth and in the presence of many witnesses, my son has professed his faith in Jesus as His Savior. When I see my believing son in sin, then I can stand in the gap in prayer for him while he struggles to come to sanity and God will give him life.

Right now my son does not understand what it takes to break free of his sin – how much soul-searching, prayer, right thinking, and healing must occur before he can break out of this bondage of addiction. I must be faithful to place him before the Lord every day and to believe God for his life.

For we are Christ's ambassadors. God is making His appeal through us.
2 Corinthians 5:20

We are like a fragrant perfume to our sons and daughters.

God says in His word that if we stand in the gap then He will give him life. God's kind of life on earth is health, happiness, joy, peace, positive words, whole relationships, love, and purpose. All of it. Nothing withheld. God tells us we have to work out our salvation with fear and trembling. The blood of Jesus and our faith in that free gift is the only pathway to salvation. But we have to walk it out in order to have what He wanted us to have on the earth.

Death is the opposite of life. Death is separation from God. It is darkness, confusion, wrong thinking, and destruction on earth leading ultimately to separation from all that is good.

God said He would give him life if I would pray. That's the Word of God and I will believe it, speak it, and live it. Praise God for life-giving words.

This book is for parents, perhaps especially for mothers. Drugs lead down a treacherous path and it doesn't always end at the rainbow. Darla battled serious depression after Nate's death. She was unable to work for six months because she simply couldn't function under the weight of the shock. But God stores up our tears because each one of them matter to Him. Little by little she was restored by keeping her eyes on the promises of God and the heart of God toward her. She became the children's church leader at the small storefront church we had both attended. She loved them and she poured her heart into her little gaggle of rowdies. Seeds of love and acceptance were sown in them. She learned to be tough when she needed to be and tender when grace needed to be applied like a healing balm. Her relationship with her daughter and her grandchildren filled her empty spots with joy and laughter. Sometimes we just have to survive until we can thrive.

Seek First to Understand

1. Recall the time and place where you first openly stood up for Jesus and told God and anyone else listening that you believed in Him.

2. If you consider yourself a person of faith, but you can't recall taking that step, do it now in your own words. Let God your Father know that you believe Jesus died for your sins and rose again so that you could be with Him in Heaven.

3. Tell God you are sorry for your sins, and you are giving your own life to Him.

4. Now tell one person about your decision to give Jesus your whole and complete life.

5. If you don't feel *good enough* to call on Jesus, you are right. None of us are. Jesus was good enough, and He took all of our punishment, guilt, and shame. Enter into freedom.

God's Word

If you confess with your mouth, "Jesus is Lord," and believe in your heart that God raised him from the dead, you will be saved.
Romans 10:9

My sheep listen to my voice; I know them, and they follow me. I give them eternal life and they shall never perish; no one can snatch them out of my hand.
John 10:27

My Prayer

Father, Thank you for giving me the freedom to choose. I choose to trust You. I believe that You love my son, that You won't give up on him, and You will continue to draw him to You. Thank you for my life and for his. In Jesus. Amen.

THE LION, THE WITCH, AND THE WARDROBE
C. S. Lewis

*"Please---Aslan," said Lucy, "can anything be done
to save Edmund?"*

*"All shall be done," said Aslan. "But it may be
harder than you think."*

CHAPTER THIRTEEN

The Roller Coaster

He has been gone less than a week and my emotions want to rule over me. The sense of relief that came from having him in a *safe place* and praising God for this was replaced by depression and anger. I tried to understand myself. I dare not yield to the full range of my feelings when in that fragile period that exists when the addict is making a decision whether to go into treatment or run away again. Only now that he was safe were those other feelings beginning to surface.

There was anger in my heart and on my face. I felt anger as I rehearsed in my mind the most recent round of lies, stealing, disrespect, and ingratitude. I felt anger and frustration about the money I wasted on college classes that were never attended. How could he? And how could I? I felt anger and disappointment in myself for having been so naïve once again.

I even felt anger toward my daughter. She is relieved to have him gone. She recognized the tremendous strain that the addiction had placed on her own marriage and how many times she had placed Josh's needs ahead of her husband's needs. I felt resentment toward her for being glad he was gone. I was not able to think rationally about this. I was a pressure cooker about to blow and there was plenty of steam to go around.

Sin separates. It separates us from God. It separates us from each other. It separates us from the good things God had intended for us. There were people in my life, but I felt lonely, an ache no one but God could fill. In a quiet moment I found this scripture, *Sooner will a mother forget the child at her breast than God will forget me.* Isaiah 49:15. Only a woman could understand. I needed this Word right at this time.

I remember breastfeeding, especially when I went back to work and my breasts were throbbing by the time I rushed home at night. There weren't a lot of nursing moms in the workplace back in the 70s and I didn't know about breast pumps. In time when I gave up on trying to nurse and work, the swelling disappeared and the pains subsided and now it's all a faint memory. But God gives women graphic pictures of His love for us. He said I might *forget* to nurse my screaming child, but He *never* stops thinking about me. He knows my foolish thinking, my tears, my heartache, and my loneliness. *Lord, please help me.* I needed what only He could supply.

In the early days when my son was in long-term rehab, God took me to Hannah's story in 1 Samuel 1 and 2. She was childless. In those days barrenness was looked upon as a punishment for sin and it brought shame on the husband of such a woman. At the temple, Hannah was in a hostile environment surrounded by the church people and she *felt* bitter disappointment. She *wept much* and she didn't eat. She was *depressed*. Her emotions were so great she was *pouring out her soul* to the Lord. Even the priest falsely accused her, misunderstanding her public display of *great anguish and grief* and accusing her of drunkenness. But then she told the priest the source of her emotional pain and Eli prophesied that God had heard her cries and she would have a son. Immediately Hannah ate and the countenance of her face changed. She no longer had even a sad look. When she knew her petition for a child had been heard by God she *stopped crying*. Later, when it was time to bring three year old Samuel to the temple to serve God, she was able to praise Him even in the separation. She was keeping the promise she made to God. There is no record of hesitation or unwillingness on her part to keep her commitment and give up her child to serve the Lord. God was showing me through Hannah's example that it's okay to feel. God gave me emotions. Hannah cried. Sometimes you just have to cry to release the pain.

God needed a trustworthy man to fill the position of high priest, because Eli had refused to deal with the sin in his sons' lives and he was going to pay the price with his own life. His own sons were not worthy to be spiritual leaders, and perhaps God chose to prepare someone from a young age. Perhaps God had closed Hannah's womb for a season in order to prepare her to sacrifice her firstborn son in the service of the Lord.

As soon as Hannah believed God was going to give her a child, she stopped crying. She didn't wait until she was pregnant, gave birth, or had other children. God was showing me that I had to get my emotions in line with my faith and it needed to show up on my face. Praise changes emotions. Hannah began to worship the Lord as soon as she believed God. I began to praise God for saving my son's life and giving him an abundant life. I praised Him for all that He would do in my own life, remembering how many painful situations He had brought me through in the past. I needed to take a kingdom view of my circumstances. If Hannah had not been childless for so long she would not have been so thankful and so willing to leave Samuel at the temple. Similarly, I had to take a kingdom view of my son's life. Samuel was raised up to take over the spiritual leadership of Israel when Eli's sons failed. He was a great man of God who saw the nation through challenging times. He anointed David, from whose lineage would come Jesus the Christ. What was I believing about Josh's future?

Was I willing to let my son go to serve God's purposes, even when I didn't know what those purposes were? Five years earlier I had written *Josh* next to Isaiah 44:5, *still another will write on his hand, ''The Lord's' and will take the name Israel.* Hannah might have smothered Samuel with her love if she had kept him by her side always. God might not have blessed her with several other children if she had not been willing to offer her firstborn to God. Samuel learned his first lesson about service to God from his mother's example. Twelve months later when Josh told me he would not be moving back to the Midwest, but would stay in Florida where he was safer, I rejoiced. His life was so precious to me, and I truly trusted God to provide for him and use him there.

Seek First to Understand

1. Look back at how far God has brought you since your own decision to follow Jesus. How have you changed?

2. What gifts and talents do you see in your child that God could use?

3. Can you see each step that is needed in your child's life in order to make him a useful vessel? Do you believe God can see what he needs even more than you do?

4. Put soft praise music on. Make a list of five things you are thankful for today.

God's Word

Blessed is the man that feareth the Lord, that delighteth greatly in His commandments.
His seed shall be mighty upon the earth;
the generation of the upright shall be blessed.
Psalm 112:1-2

I will pour my spirit upon thy seed, and my blessing upon thine offspring.
Isaiah 44:3

"As for me, this is my covenant with them," saith the Lord
"My spirit that is upon thee, and my words which I have put in thy mouth
shall not depart out of thy mouth, nor out of the mouth of thy seed
nor out of the mouth of thy seed's seed," saith the Lord, "from henceforth and forever."
Isaiah 59:21

Be still, and know that I am God.
Psalm 46:10

Prayer

Father, Thank You for quieting my heart and reminding me of the things You have promised for my son. Thank You for keeping him alive. Thank You for the gifts and talents you have given him and for the unique personality he has. I believe that he will serve You, and I know that You are the only one who can prepare him for the assignment you have for him. You know the people you need to bring into his life. You know what he needs to experience. I praise You for Your great love for him and for training him. In Jesus. Amen.

THE LION, THE WITCH, AND THE WARDROBE
C. S. Lewis

"I've come at last," said he. "She has kept me out for a long time, but I have got in at last. Aslan is on the move. The Witch's magic is weakening."

And Lucy felt running through her that deep shiver of gladness which you only get if you are being solemn and still.

CHAPTER FOURTEEN

From Death to Life

Women received their dead back to life
Hebrews 11:35

I know a woman who lived 3,000 years ago. I don't know her name, but she had a profound impact on me. The Shunammite woman was a woman of character, a generous woman, and a follower of God. She was married to a man of wealth who was much older than her, probably an arranged marriage. She was childless in a day when a woman's identity was determined by the productivity of her womb. She was past her childbearing years.

During her lifetime, recorded in II Kings 4 and 8, God spoke to His people only through His prophets. These men heard from God, reported from God, and inquired of God. Elisha was an old prophet who had served the Lord well. He lived in Gilgal but frequently traveled 60 miles to Mount Carmel, where he communed with Most High God. When he reached Shunem he still had 20 more miles to ride his donkey or walk. With a heart to serve, the Shunammite woman invited him to dinner as he traveled through her town. Eventually she asked her husband's permission to make a room for him so that he could always have a place to rest as he made his spiritual pilgrimage.

Elisha wanted to bless her in response to her generosity. He inquired of her need but she said she already had everything she needed. Elisha's servant Gehazi quietly told his master that she was without child, and with a word from God, Elisha promised her a son. Instead of being grateful, the Shunammite woman was angry. She believed it impossible and thought the prophet was just one more cruel person making sport of her barren womb. Nevertheless, God is faithful to His word, and she had a baby boy.

A few years later the boy became ill and died in her arms. But the Shunammite woman had changed. She was now a woman of faith not unbelief. She placed his body on the bed of Elisha and set out across the desert on a donkey to find the man of God. Her husband asked, *What's wrong? ... Nothing,* she replied. She approached Mount Carmel. Gehazi the servant of Elisha ran to her. *What's wrong?* he asked. *...Nothing.* The words of unbelief would not come again from her mouth. Only when she was at the feet of Elisha did she collapse in agony at his feet. He instantly felt her bitter pain. It was the boy. He knew. He was old and slow. Time was critical. When he tried to send her on ahead with his servant, she uttered these profound words, "As surely as the Lord lives and as you live, I will not leave you."

They rode together as fast as two people can move on a slow, tired donkey across the desert. They arrived. God moved through Elisha and the boy was restored to life. The woman received her dead back to life.

A famine began, and Elisha told her to leave with her family for a time. She obeyed. Seven years after they left Israel, the drought was over and she reappeared. This time she had only her son. Her husband had died. A woman did not go before the King alone, and her son was by her side while they met with the King. Inspired by the resurrection testimony, he restored her land and seven years of produce....in other words, all her wealth. In Hebrews Chapter 11 it is assumed by scholars that the woman spoken of as a great woman of faith was the Shunammite woman.

How did she change this much? Despite the culture that regarded women as slightly above animals, the spokesman for God knew that women, too, were made in the image of God and deserved to be taught. When the man of God was with her in her home from the beginning, he saw that she did not understand the power of the God she honored with her works. But he was not dismayed. He must have taught her each time he stayed at her house. He taught and she listened. Clearly, this child she wasn't supposed to have was in her arms, and the promises of God had taken on new meaning to her. Year after year Elisha stayed. She fed him, served him, and hung on every word.

When her moment of desperation came, she now put into practice all that she had been taught. Do not speak unbelief. Pour your heart out only to God. Know how much He loves you. Believe God's power. Above all else, don't leave the side of God. Put Him first always and trust Him to overcome insurmountable obstacles.

After I read her story, I adopted Hebrews 11:35 as a key scripture to proclaim over my son. No matter what it looked like to the outside world, no matter who said what, my son will live and not die. My son will be delivered out of the death trap of drugs into new life.

God knew she would need a son, even when she didn't know. God knows what I need even when I don't know. If I will stay by God's side and never leave Him out of any of my situations, He will do miracles for me and my boy.

Seek First to Understand

1. What miracle do you need today? Write it down.

2. How has God shown his power in your life? Name one significant example.

3. Read about the Shunammite woman in 2 Kings 4:8-37 and 8:1-6. What did she speak about her son's death? To whom? What was God's response?

God's Word

But you are near, O Lord, and all your commands are true.
Psalm 119:151

Go and announce to them that the Kingdom of Heaven is near.
Matthew 10:7

Who can list the glorious miracles of the Lord?
Who can ever praise him enough?
Psalm 106:2

Remember the wonders he has performed, his miracles,
and the rulings he has given.
Psalm 105:5

Prayer

Lord, I ask your forgiveness for the words of unbelief I have listened to and spoken over my child. You are faithful. You have pulled my life from the mud. You have saved my child's life again and again. _____ is the miracle I'm asking for in your timing and in your way. I believe you will do it. My child will live and not die. We will both draw near to you and grow up in Christ. I know you are still in the miracle business. I rest in your healing presence. Amen.

CHAPTER FIFTEEN

My Race

I was attending a conference for Christian women in Orange Beach, Louisiana. From the moment the main speaker opened her mouth, she had my attention. She had been teaching for two days from Hebrews 12...*let us throw off everything that hinders and the sin that so easily entangles, and let us run the race marked out for us.* Close your eyes for a moment, she instructed, and eighty women obeyed. She read the scripture slowly, and she encouraged us to picture ourselves fulfilling the dream, the call, the vision that God had given us for a fulfilling, powerful life. What kind of person did we see fulfilling that vision? What strengths? What confidence? I saw myself traveling the world, praying for women and teaching women in other nations. I saw myself totally equipped by God to go and do what He had beckoned me to do.

Without a breath between, our speaker suddenly said *Now open your eyes and quickly write in your journal three things that are keeping you from fulfilling that vision.* The first thing I wrote was *Josh.* The harsh truth hit me once again. I was still so enmeshed in his physical, mental, and spiritual condition that I was hindered from doing what God had created me to do.

This exercise would stay with me forever. God had brought me so far. Ten years earlier when separated from my husband of 25 years, I had completed a 12-step recovery program. I had labored for nine months alongside 15 other women and men whose lives were completely messed up. Only three of us made it to the very end of the program. We were the very desperate, determined three who just had to get healed of what sickened our hearts. We battled to understand why we had stayed in abusive relationships, how we had been molded by our birth families, and most importantly how to take back control of our own lives. We had made our peace with God and begun to learn how to pray. We made some amends to people we had harmed. We experimented with laughter we did not think we deserved to enjoy. We shared secrets we had just learned about ourselves. And we gave each other strength and encouragement to change our behaviors, our choices, and our lives.

Honest self-examination is like peeling back an onion. It isn't smooth. It comes off in chunks to reveal the next layer that must be peeled. And it makes you cry. But after each painful step you get closer to the good stuff. You give what you have peeled off to God because you can't put it back together again and you don't know what else to do with it. He sheds His light on the pieces that made you cry and reminds you that you are the good stuff in His eyes.

After five years in court, my divorce was final and I thought I might die. Anguish poured out of my eyes as I peeled my garden of stinking onions. But I didn't die. God changed me a day at a time. I learned to be honest and develop good relationships with my children. I found a church family who helped my kids and me feel accepted. I learned to stand up to intimidators with calm strength that rendered them unable to hurt me. I learned to buy and sell houses and cars and do the necessary things that a single mother has to do. I stopped being sick all the time. And I learned to walk down the street with my head up, no longer feeling unworthy or ashamed to be me.

Now here I was a decade later dealing with addiction again in another generation and peeling back another layer. Yes, I was healthier in so many ways. On the outside I looked great! I had a good job. I was attractive. We lived in a pretty house. I was a regular church-goer. But this question made me cry deep inside my soul. If I did not learn to trust God with my son and believe His promises and His love toward Josh and toward me, how could I complete the purpose for which I was created? This was devastating

In this moment I was faced with the ugliness of my own unbelief that the Creator of each of us is fully trustworthy to deal with my child in the way He knows best. With every addiction, we who love them can get drawn into the delusion that we can fix them if we just love them enough or find the right formula. The One who understands our hearts divides soul and spirit and deals with our motives.

This day I resolve once again to enter the Sabbath-rest of God (Hebrews 4), to peel back the layers and give the peelings to the One who watches over me. In order to enter this place of continual rest, I must give *myself* to God. I must open my ears to hear and eyes to see what He wants me to do for others as an outward expression of my love for Him and His love for me. What I have learned about the Sabbath rest in times of fear, rejection, and anguish is for a purpose. God wants to use the pain to help women both in my back yard and in other nations. I must live the only life I can live…my own.

Seek First to Understand

1. What life experiences have you had that God could use to help others through the same traumas?

2. What preparation would you need in order to help others?

3. Colossians 1:16 says that we are created by Jesus and for Jesus. Knowing that there is no DNA like yours and that you have been placed here at this exact time, what thoughts have you ever had about the reason why he created you?

4. What keeps you from running the race set before you?

God's Word

Even before He made the world, God loved us and chose us in Christ
to be holy and without fault in his eyes.
Ephesians 1:4

As each part does its own special work, it helps the other parts grow
Ephesians 4:16

When we ourselves are comforted, we will certainly comfort you.
2 Corinthians 1:6

It is not that we think we are qualified to do anything on our own. Our qualification comes from God. He has enabled us to be ministers of his new covenant.
2 Corinthians 3:5-6

For the promise of entering God's rest still stands.
For all who have entered into God's rest
have rested from their labors, just as God did after creating the world
Hebrews 4:1 and 10.

Prayer

Lord, you had a plan for me before You created the world. You qualify me to use the gifts that You have put in me to bring You glory and honor. That is what I want. I have allowed myself to get so entangled with the life of my child that I have lost sight of my own. I need your help to get free of the burden of carrying another person's life. Please show me how to do this and see it with Your eyes. Let me enter your resting place. I love You, God. Amen

THE LION, THE WITCH, AND THE WARDROBE
C. S. Lewis

There is no need to tell you (and no one ever heard) what Aslan was saying but it was a conversation which Edmund never forgot. As the others drew nearer, Aslan turned to meet them, bringing Edmund with him.

CHAPTER SIXTEEN

Hurricanes, Sharks & Snakes! Oh My!

The fruit of righteousness will be peace, the effect of righteousness
will be quiet confidence forever. My people will live in peaceful dwelling places,
in secure homes, in undisturbed places of rest.
Isaiah 32:17-18

At last! He is in a safe place. My friend said, *I never worried about them when they were in the rehab center, only after they got out.* Right, right. I can relax. After one month I am beginning to sleep a little better. The phone calls from his dad, his siblings, and true friends are less frequent, less strained. Our conversations still center around him, wondering how he's doing, but we are also venturing back into the forgotten corners of our own lives. It feels so good to go out with friends, to make personal plans, to think about my own aspirations for the first time in a long time. I had forgotten what *normal* feels like.

Then as slowly as that peace began to drift in, the unsettling reports began to lap like high tide....shark attacks in the area he is living in. One fatality, another amputation. Darla and I had dropped him off in August. In September, hurricane season started. Hurricane Ivan was bearing down on the Panhandle of Florida and the eye was headed directly to Sandestin. Now what, God? I thought he was going to be safe there. Can he be safe anywhere?

Suddenly the phone rang at 10 p.m. It was him. Still not allowed phone privileges, he borrowed a cell phone for just a brief moment to call Mom. If he got caught using a phone he could get kicked out. But it was urgent. *We're in a hurricane,* he said. *We didn't evacuate. The winds are roaring.* He didn't say he was frightened, but I could hear it in his voice. I assured him that God was watching over him. I said, *Pray* and he said, *Oh I am!* And I said, *I am in prayer for you* and that was what he needed to hear.

I'm up! I'm praying! I'm pacing. I'm calling his Dad...get up out of bed and pray for your son! I make calls to the sisters and to a couple of friends. Pray! I stay up most of the night watching the weather, in prayer vigil with my son, and yet peaceful. Once again God was giving me an unfamiliar peace. It was not the eye of the hurricane but the eye of the Living God that had my son in its sights. The hurricane turned west at the last hour and the rehabilitation center was spared. Three more hurricanes came his way in the next 12 months, and each one passed him by.

Two months later when he was officially allowed to contact us, we learned that he stayed out of the shark infested waters and had also learned to bypass scorpions and snakes that wanted to share his room. I was not there to warn him, to make a suggestion, to remind him to be careful. He overcame his fears and moved an inch toward manhood. My safety net of protection had never worked when he lived under my roof. Only God knows the pit that lies before us, and when it's necessary to let us fall in and when to enable us to sidestep it.

Seek First to Understand

Codependent: Unhealthy psychological reliance of one person on another. Addicted, attached, hooked, interconnected, interdependent, mutually dependent, slavish trust, unhealthy confidence.

Do you recognize yourself in any of these descriptors? All of them?

Rest. See yourself in a cozy log cabin in the mountains. You are in a large wooden rocker gazing at a gentle stream bubbling off the front porch. A patchwork quilt is snuggled over your lap. A mug of steaming lavender tea sits on a small shabby chic table at your right side. The chill fall air brings the scent of the woods to life, along with your soul. There is no cable, no wi-fi, no landline, no technology. You told no one where you were going. You booked the cabin for two weeks. You are totally, blissfully alone. You and God. Your Bible is open on your lap. You are perfectly safe and at peace.

Now imagine the usual chaos is happening back at home. How is your son reacting to your absence? What are your other children doing when they find they can't contact you? What might God be working on with each one of them? With you?

> **Freedom: Independence, license to do as one wants. Abandon, ability, bent, carte blanche, discretion, elbowroom, exemption.**

How does *freedom* look to you?

What would you be pursuing if you were free of responsibility for your son? What abilities have lain dormant? What dry bones are waiting for you to speak life?

God's Word

Read Psalm 139. This is how God thinks about you.
Meditate on verses 7-9:

> *Where can I go from your Spirit? Where can I flee from your presence?*
> *If I go up to the heavens - you are there. If I make my bed in the depths - you are there.*
> *If I rise on the wings of the dawn, if I settle on the far side of the sea,*
> *even there your hand will guide me, your right hand will hold me fast.*

Read those verses again. Apply them to your child. Apply them to your other children. Apply them to yourself. Start or continue to keep a journal about what God reveals to you.

Prayer

Lord, you are with me everywhere I go. You think about me constantly. When I abide in you I am at perfect peace. You want me to live in freedom. Forgive me, Lord, when I fail to trust you with my children. You brought me through the testing times and you will do the same for them.

Let me live a full and abundant life, using all the gifts you put in me when you knit me together in my mother's womb. Help me to unwrap my fingers and let my child make his choices. I am not his rescuer. You are. For today, for this moment, I set us both free. In Christ, Amen.

CHAPTER SEVENTEEN

It's Beginning to Rain

Elijah now prayed for the drought to end. Three years earlier he had prayed for the drought to begin, to demonstrate the power of God to a stubborn people. The time of drought brought bitter resentment toward this prophet of God. Condemnation. Death threats. But he had endured. Now it was time for rain. He prayed and sent the messenger. Anything? No, not yet. Seven times he repeated his command to the messenger. Then a cloud as big as a man's fist appeared on the horizon. A weaker man might not have understood the significance of this small white wisp. But Elijah knew that a storm was coming and the drought would end.

The first wisp appeared while my son and I were sitting on a broken step leading down to the beach. A weekday in January found only a few sojourners on this stretch of beach heavily damaged by recent hurricanes. This was my first personal visit with my son in five months. He had passed through the time of mandatory separation from all contact with family. Now he was allowed to invite only me, and I had arranged to come down for a short visit. We had gotten past a few uncomfortable times together and awkward silences. We were able to spend time with each other feeling the warmth of familial love for the first time in a very very long time. He needed to chitchat about life in the Center. Nicknames of his new brothers: *Quick John* for his quick temper. *Big*...for an overeater. Josh is cooking for 30 guys *with love* and entrusted with the weekly SAMS grocery trip.

Suddenly amidst the talk of daily life he was pacing near me. He began to tell me how sorry he was for the pain he had caused me. Oh, this was it. He was beginning the process of Step 8 – making amends. A quick silent prayer, *Oh, God, help me to respond right.* I avoided eye contact but listened intently as he let me know that he really understood that a mother's pain is not the financial loss or the sting of embarrassment, but the fear that grips us when we don't know if they will make it home tonight. For the first time, I heard true repentance. The honest admission that the only way he could make it right was to live right and salvage his life. I had left a frightened boy behind five months ago, and I was hearing the voice of a man on a pilgrimage to find himself.

Amazing grace is more than a familiar song. It flows through us toward a fellow traveler. As the words were leaving his mouth I was receiving this new person as another adult who had struggled to overcome the grip of sin. A strong hand from heaven reached down to clip off the iron apron strings. He was free to choose his life, and his sincere intention was to triumph over his past and be what God created him to be. I was free to choose my life, and to love him with abandon…no requirements.

The clouds have grown bigger over the months since that day. Each month a new milestone is gained. Working 40 hours a week. Paying for his own care at the Center. A repayment plan worked out for items stolen to buy drugs. Paying for his own car insurance and getting his car back. Initiation of an improved relationship with his father. Making a realistic next-step plan for his life. The fruit of the Spirit is popping up and being noticed. Acts of kindness. Generosity. Other-centeredness.

The smell of rain is in the air.

Seek First to Understand

1. Read the story of Elijah in 1 Kings 17-19. Take note of:
   The unstable people in his life
   The forces of evil coming against him
   His own ups and downs of emotion and the times he ran away
       from the conflicts in his life
   The miracles God did through him during the drought

2. Is there a wisp of cloud on your horizon anywhere? What is it?

3. If your first reaction was *No, nothing* look again. Can you see anything?

4. What miracle are you awaiting? Focus on that wisp of hope in God's power to work healing in your child's life. Journal about it or write it here.

5. What will you have to do to survive the drought in the meantime?

God's Word

The seventh time the servant reported,
'A cloud as small as a man's hand is rising from the sea.'
1 Kings 18:44

Prayer

My Father in Heaven, thank you for sending me hope. I see a glimpse of change, one good thing. I trust you. I know that you are working on a miraculous life change for my child. You have done a miracle in my own life. I am not the same person I once was. It seems like a very slow process, but you have been so patient with me. Let me be patient with my child and with your timing. During the drought, Lord, please help me to love and serve others who need your touch. I want to keep my focus on you, and I need your help to do that today. In Jesus. Amen.

CHAPTER EIGHTEEN

Friends and Other Snake Holes

Tonight I went to the funeral visitation of Bobby, the 26 year old neighbor who was dealing drugs at the age of 18. He supplied drugs to my 14 year old son and many other teens. Around the room were photos of him as an innocent young towheaded boy with grandma. Also around the room were photos of him partying, many with a beer in his hand. He died on New Years Day at 6:30 a.m. after drinking in a bar in downtown St. Louis. Four miles from his dad's home in my old neighborhood he rolled his car over several times and died.

I went there to represent my son, in recovery 850 miles away, who was sick at heart over this death. He described Bobby as full of life, a person who loved people, a person with a good heart who would have helped others if he had ever been able to defeat the addiction demon. Josh surmised even though the papers didn't report it, that his death was alcohol related. A mutual friend had said that Bobby was drinking and drugging again. Though they may not talk often, Josh and his old running buddies always talk about the status of sobriety or lack of among their old buds. News frightens them. They know the devastation and sincerely hope each will miraculously overcome. In the ten years I have known this family, Bobby has been sent away to military school, to out of state rehabilitation, to jail, under house arrest, in court, and in trouble.

There was a time when I felt hatred for this whole family because I blamed them for delivering drugs to my son, for covering up for him, for hiding him in their home, for teenage drinking parties with full involvement of their parents. There's so much blame to go around. Yet tonight all I could think about was the tremendous sadness of wasted lives. Bobby's hope of a normal life is over at 26. Little Brother Kerry was perilously hanging onto sobriety. His mother quickly told me that Kerry has been sober for seven months. This is how we measure success. It isn't whether they are educated, happily married with a good career, but only measured in months of sobriety. The family dysfunction is evident. Dad was stoic and business-like, pretending like he always did that this was no big deal. Mom, always trying to be like one of the kids, tells me that *this sucks* when I walk up to her to express my sorrow. Her talk is of herself and her new marriage.

She let me know immediately that Bobby was a Christian. I believe this to be true. I remember he and Josh attending a men's conference at my church and both going forward, desperately seeking deliverance. But at the same time I wonder if it's good or bad that she feels she needs to say this to me immediately. Is my Christian *reputation* one of judgment and condemnation or one of love? I want it to be one of love. There is no room for judgment in my life. Oh but for the grace of God this would be my son and my heartache. How grateful I am to be spared this agony.

Yet how angry I feel at Satan for stealing the life of that young tow-headed boy next to his grandma in the picture. I scan a roomful of young men now in their twenties, vaguely recognizing many who ran with my boy. Many are crying. Others are biting back tears but fear is written on their faces. Oh God help them and help their parents. Help me to be faithful to pray for my own son and never stop fighting the battle of the spirit in prayer. We know that our choices have consequences but when I see the consequences and the suffering of the innocent young it makes me want to scream.

Our only hope is God in Christ.

Josh has buried other friends. Some from rehab centers they cohabited. One, a fellow heroin addict in Tulsa who OD'd. His shared needle infected my son with Hepatitis C and the fear of that almost cost Josh his life soon after the funeral. Our only hope is God in Christ. Otherwise we are all utterly ruined.

Thank you, God, that my son is living in Florida not near the old crowd. Thank you for his life. Thank you for my life. Every day is a gift. Our only hope is God in Christ.

Seek First to Understand

1. Write the names of three of your son's drug-using friends.

2. Think about their lives, their families. Do any of them come from stable, two-parent homes? Is either biological parent an alcoholic or abusing prescription drugs? Is there a history of anger or violence? Did any of them seem love-starved? Are you aware of any physical or emotional abuse in the family? Were there any strong relationships with solid, Godly men?

3. Without placing blame on yourself or any of these families, can you spot any patterns of factors which might contribute to a child drawn to the feel-good-about-yourself allure of alcohol or drugs?

4. In Christ, you have been given the gift of the Holy Spirit. Through the eyes of the Spirit, see each of them as Jesus sees them. Write down what you see.

5. Through the eyes of the Spirit, see yourself as Jesus sees you. Write down what you see.

6. Speak words of forgiveness, adding their names. Pray for each one. Let your heart heal.

God's Word

When he saw the crowds, he had compassion on them because they were
harassed and helpless, like sheep without a shepherd.
The harvest is plentiful but the workers are few.
Ask the Lord of the harvest, therefore, to send out workers into his harvest field.
Matthew 9:36-37

124

Praise be to the God and Father of our Lord Jesus Christ, the Father of compassion
and the God of all comfort, who comforts us in all our troubles,
so that we can comfort those in any trouble
with the comfort we ourselves have received from God.
2 Corinthians 1:3-4

Prayer

God my Father, you have had compassion toward me. Time and again you have dredged me out of the mess I have dug for myself. You forgave my parents and you forgave me. Through your eyes I see the hurt in these children's lives. I also see the heartache in the family for these children they love. We are all in need of your loving compassion. Please send someone to speak life to ＿＿＿＿＿＿, ＿＿＿＿＿＿, and ＿＿＿＿＿＿. Let them know you love and forgive them. Remind me today of your love for me. My own shame was nailed to the Cross and I carry it no more. In Christ, Amen.

CHAPTER NINETEEN

Michael's Story

The opening scene in the movie *Jaws* shows a girl being whipped back and forth. Under the water a shark is biting her in half. Divorce, alcoholism, and anger among the parents wreaks that kind of havoc on the emotional development of innocent babies. They reluctantly emerge, expecting a secure life like they had in the womb.

How many funerals will I attend from among Josh's old friends? Only God knows. He and Michael have been friends for 27 years since they were six year old first graders. It has been a friendship that has put my teeth on edge. Nothing good ever seemed to come of it. I was one of those moms who never threw away any school paper. Recently I was cleaning out the seven tubs of old school papers and I came across one Michael had written to Josh. *I will either be in jail or in hell.* He had been to jail several times. But for the grace of God my son wasn't with him. I took that paper outside and burned it.

My son introduced Michael to heroin. I am nauseated by the thought of it. John 10:10 *the devil comes to steal, kill, and destroy.* So many people today don't believe that Satan is real but whether you do or not, no one who has been near the drug scene would argue that the spider's web traps you without warning. Josh has struggled with guilt and shame over that and stayed connected to Michael even when he knew nothing good could come of it.

Three times this week I have been to the hospital to hold vigil with Michael's mother as he fights for his life. In Missouri Baptist Hospital, one of the largest in St. Louis, the doctor said Michael is the sickest patient they have. Admitted only a week ago with an unexplained pain in his shoulder, he now lies in an induced coma, with a breathing tube down his throat forcing air into his collapsed lungs. Two blood clots are near his heart. A staph infection of the worst kind is raging through his body. Fever causes him to be packed in ice. Immobilization, weakness, nausea. Tubes are running in and out of his young body. He is struggling with the sickness caused by opiate withdrawal while his vital organs are attacked by an infection probably introduced by a needle.

His 24 year old wife of only two months sits daily by his side, signing consent forms for his medical procedures and wondering how she is going to provide for their four year old daughter with a sick husband and no income and her own family a thousand miles away. There is no talk of the hundreds of thousands of dollars this care will cost the hospital and ultimately the taxpayers, as Michael is among the nation's many uninsured. The users who try to convince themselves that they are only harming themselves should be in this room right now, watching the haunted expressions on the faces of those who didn't really want to admit to themselves that he was using again, even though the evidence was overwhelming.

These two had stolen together. Josh had OD'd in their living room and had to be resuscitated. Michael's mother had snorted cocaine with them in her home while attending Bible studies with me and lying to me about what was happening. For five years I was so angry with Michael and his family that I refused to speak with them. During that five years he went away to prison twice for drug-related crimes and out again, always with the sincere pronouncement that he was done with this and would never again use drugs. For my part, it was self-protection. I needed to heal, and I needed distance between anyone associated with my son's old drug life and my life. Now here I am standing alongside the family praying for his survival, asking God for His mercy once again. I feel no anger toward a particular person now, only intense sorrow for the family. The things I learned while fighting in prayer for my son's life will now be put to use in helping another mother fight for her son's life.

Unforgiveness poisons the person who carries it. I have struggled with this for forty years. It was easy to excuse myself, especially when I focused on my childhood. I was sexually abused and denied some basic needs like medical and dental care, warm or decent clothing, and heated shelter. Poverty carries its own sense of shame. It was an easy slide into marriage with another victim of deprivation and the added complexity of generational alcoholism. Out of his wounded heart came words that twisted the knife in my own wounded heart. For the first 40 years I did not understand that *the problem wasn't him or them*. All of my emotional issues did not go away after the divorce. Awareness that I might be *the issue* was followed slowly by acknowledgement that I needed to change if I wanted to live free. We are told in God's word to *work out our salvation.*

Our salvation is a free gift made available by Jesus' blood sacrifice. But this process of becoming more Christ-like means I have to walk it out, to let the Jesus in me reign in my soul and show up on the outside.

In <u>My Spiritual Journey</u>, the 12-step recovery program I waded through in nine months with 15 other people, I started to peel back the onion. I had to choose to remember the painful details of my childhood and then to see the same human condition in my parents as there was in me. We were all sinners in need of a savior. At the right time and in exactly the right way, God orchestrated the confrontation with each member of my family that I felt had harmed me. It came in stages and those open talks were often separated by years as God prepared my heart and theirs for healing, a.k.a. forgiveness. The very exercise of being honest and opening the cage door of my wounded feelings was a giant leap toward that forgiveness. As I forgave them I was more able to see my own part in the breakdown of our relationships. I had held onto my anger like a well-worn blankie. I was used to living with it. I felt comfortable in my victimization. Less was required of me if I kept my eyes on them, or so I mistakenly thought.

Twelve years later I signed up for another step course called <u>Living in Freedom Every Day</u>. This is an area that each of us will have to revisit because offense never stops coming as long as we draw breath and interact with others. It is important to learn what forgiveness is not. It is not minimizing the offense. It is a serious thing for an adult to participate with a child in drug use or to deliberately hide it from that child's parent. What was done was not right, but when I choose to forgive, I choose not to hang onto the offense because it robs me of freedom. Forgiveness is not reconciliation. The last time I permitted Michael into my home he was high on heroin and came only to try to get money from my son. He is still using and now dealing. It is wisdom to say *No* to involvement with this family until such time the Holy Spirit shows me that it will not harm me or my family. If I wait until they are well or have asked for forgiveness from me, I am still leaving my freedom to another person. Forgiveness is not forgetting what happened. I may never forget what happened. But God wants to heal my heart so that I can remember it without the pain. He has done that for me with my father and my ex-husband and others. I have to give even the drug-related relationships to him so that my heart is healed.

Step two of any step program is that we come to believe there is a power higher than us who can help us do what we don't believe we can do. The Bible says that someone is Jesus. Step three is my willingness to give up what I have perceived as *my right* to be angry and acknowledge that I am willing to let Jesus have control. *I can do all things through Christ who strengthens me.* Forgiveness does not turn us into doormats. Just the opposite occurs, we become victorious. When I learned to stand up to the bullies in my life they immediately stopped trying to use those tactics. I felt empowered for the first time in my life.

I continued to read books about forgiveness. Two that helped me the most were <u>Forgiveness</u> by Charles Stanley and <u>The Bait of Satan</u> by John Bevere. The word *offense* comes from the Greek word *scandalon* which means *the bait*. Our enemy sets bait to lure us into the trap of unforgiveness and lost intimacy with God. Years later I soaked up Dr. Caroline Leaf's teaching in <u>Who Switched Off My Brain.</u> This wonderful brain scientist helped me unlock the missing piece of just how unforgiveness and anger had affected me. In a thirty year marriage of near daily feeding of anger and unforgiveness, I had flooded my brain with a chemical overload that was toxic in its power. My toxic brain had triggered constant colds and viruses but also chronic illnesses like hypertension and rheumatoid arthritis. I had developed a stronghold in my mind that found the neurons of my brain woven into a literal nest of anger enveloped by a dark cloud of chemicals. It's who I was. I was also a person raised to believe that women were to be invisible and silent. If you spoke up you would be punished. Like a balloon waiting to pop I sucked more anger in with every offense. I was at home there. I displayed it with slammed doors or days of the silent treatment but I didn't deal with anything quickly or honestly. When I understood that I had been literally killing myself with anger, I committed myself to learning to be honest and to forgive. The good news from Dr. Leaf is that I could literally change my brain. I became consumed with this knowledge. I taught it in conferences in Europe and the U.S. The more I taught it the more I lived it.

It is an individual journey but one necessary for survival. I must make a daily choice to forgive. First choose to forgive, then your feelings follow. This bird has left the cage.

Six thousand miles away I visited a drug and alcohol rehabilitation center in Transnistria, an unofficial *country* between Ukraine & Moldova. There was a young man the age of my son named Johnny. Through a translator I told these men about Josh back home and how God was faithful to heal him and them. I hugged their unwashed, unshaven, lonely selves and I genuinely loved them. Unlike the creature comforts of most centers in America, this handful of men went to bed at dusk because they had no electricity for light. Their days were spent caring for small animals and tending the garden so they would have food. Each man had a bed and one extra shirt hanging on a nail near the bed. Heat was a wood-burning stove in the rudimentary kitchen area. In the winter they were always cold.

A local pastor came weekly to teach them and bring some food from the church families. I wrote a fundraising appeal letter on behalf of the ministry to help build a comfortable center there. God used there what I have lived through here. God will use it but He didn't cause it. Years later the center is comfortable and thriving and men are being set free to return to their families.

May God have mercy on us all as we depend on Him to save us and to continue to pick us up from the floor when we stumble. Let us not judge another. We all have sinned and fallen short of the glory of God. It is impossible to forgive others until we receive forgiveness for ourselves. God loves you and me. He sacrificed his son so that we could be cleansed. What we have been given we are called to give others. Love bears all things. We will bear with our children when they cannot help themselves and pray fervently that God will give those in the struggle, including his still-using friends, another chance to heal and forgive.

Seek First to Understand

1. Is there anyone in your past or present from whom you have withheld forgiveness?

2. If God our Father was describing this person to you, smiling as if in fond remembrance, what favorite things would He mention?

3. List three things you know about this person's past that could have caused them to react to you or others in such unloving ways.

4. See yourself as God sees you. Memorize this verse and speak it over yourself daily: *I am the righteousness of God in Christ.*

God's Word

And forgive us our sins as we forgive those who have sinned against us.
Matthew 6:12

God saved you by his grace when you believed.
And you can't take credit for this; it is a gift from God.
Ephesians 2:8

Look after each other so that none of you fails to receive the grace of God. Watch out
that no poisonous root of bitterness grows up to trouble you, corrupting many.
Hebrews 12:15

Prayer

Father, it is by your grace that I am saved. It is by your grace that my child is alive today. Let me not fail to extend grace to the injured ones so beaten up by life. I lift up _____ and ask that you help me to forgive them. Lead me along that journey until I am free from the cage. Let me bring comfort to another as I have been comforted. In Christ, Amen.

CHAPTER TWENTY

The Abundant Life

*The devil comes to steal, kill, and destroy, but I have come
that you might have life and have it more abundantly.*
John 10:10

The person of Jesus Christ. All throughout God's communication
to us He instilled hope in those who would receive hope. He told
us over and over that the Messiah was coming, then that He had come,
that He would come again, and that this One Life would enable us to
experience the love of God and the blessings of God in a way we had not
ever imagined.

Eight years ago early in the mornings, I frequently walked around
a mossy pond with my scripture cards in my hand. I was fighting for my
son's life and for my own freedom from fear. As I meditated on

John 10:10, I began to visualize and then vocalize what an *abundant life* would look like for this child of mine. Some sons are born into the Cleaver family. Everyone is respectful all the time. Minor problems are amicably resolved among family members. The athletic, bright children grow up to become world-changers and to continue the legacy of happy successful Cleavers spawning another generation of happy successful Cleavers who make a lasting contribution to the world. To my natural mind and the observation of anyone who knew us, that seemed unattainable for my son. He had squeaked through *alternative* high school, a place where they put the teenage mommies and the misfit boys who got so far off track they didn't know there was a track. He was in and out of trouble, had no healthy relationships, and was shooting heroin between his toes.

But to God nothing is impossible, and so I decided to lay hold of this promise that His Son had made. An abundant life for my son looked like good health, a career (not just a job), a wife and children, and a ministry through which God's kingdom purposes were fulfilled. I began to thank God for doing it, even though the evidence hadn't surfaced yet. The route to get there would not be ordinary because his life had not been ordinary.

Fast forward eight years. He lives in a resort community in the Panhandle of Florida, where he stayed after one year in a residential treatment program. He works part-time as a coffee roaster at a coffee shop and this provides his medical insurance. He owns a T-shirt printing business with a loyal and growing clientele among the many tourist attractions and restaurants along 30-A. He has two employees. He pays all his own bills, insures himself, drives a decent paid-off car, takes nicer vacations than I take, and keeps a small stock portfolio. Some parents might not be excited that their son prints t-shirts and brews coffee, but I praise a Mighty God because to me this is my personal miracle.

His relationship with his dad has greatly improved. He seems to know how to keep healthy boundaries and to distance himself from people who could harm him. He is willing and able to counsel others who are struggling with addictions without enabling them.

Four years ago he married Avaka, a young woman from Slovakia. Ten years ago they met while working at Starbucks together. She is not ordinary. She speaks several languages, has a B.S. in Accounting from Florida State University and other degrees she obtained in Slovakia. Is she a quiet little church girl from the Midwest US of A? Not at all. But she loves my son and he loves her. Having grown up very modestly in post-Communist Europe, she is not overly materialistic. She laughs easily. She's easy to please. They have traveled to Europe to meet the rest of her family. Their circle of friends are from nations all over the world. God is working out His plan.

They own two homes near the bay. They live in one and rent out the second. Matthew joined the family in 2012. He is healthy and beautiful. I watch my son kissing him over and over, very protectively. My God is so good.

Every aspect of the *abundant life* hasn't yet appeared. But the cloud as big as a man's fist is beginning to appear on the horizon and rain is on the way. From where we started to where we are is glorious. Can you dare to have hope when you have been so disappointed so many times? The choice to give up hoping leads to depression and an open door to that thief who wants to suck the life out of us. But the little flicker of hope can grow and sustain us when we allow ourselves to see His promises coming to pass and choose to speak them out of our mouths and into our hearts. If you can believe that Jesus was telling the truth when He made that promise, then it can become a reality in your own life and in your child's life.

Seek First to Understand

1. How do you picture *an abundant life* for your son or daughter?

2. Write it down. What might he be doing? How do you imagine God might use those unique gifts in your child? What will his relationships be like? His finances? His health? Now begin to pray and ask God for those specific blessings. Notice when those things happen one step at a time and praise God.

God's Word

If someone aspires to be an elder he desires an honorable position.
So an elder must be a man whose life is above reproach. He must be faithful to his wife.
He must exercise self-control, live wisely, and have a good reputation.
He must enjoy having guests in his home, and he must be able to teach.
He must not be a heavy drinker or be violent.
He must be gentle, not quarrelsome, and not love money. He must manage his own
family well, having children who respect and obey him.
Also people outside the church must speak well of him so that
he will not be disgraced and fall into the devil's trap.
I Timothy 3:1-4 and 7

Prayer

Our Father in Heaven, I come to you in the Name of Your Son Jesus Christ. Jesus said that Satan has been trying to kill my child. But you also said that Jesus came so that my child, _____ could have an abundant life. The little flicker of hope that I have is in that promise. I'm asking You right now to bring him the abundant life Jesus promised. I believe that _____ 's life will include _____, and _____, and _____.

I believe You have a plan for _____ that is greater than anything I could imagine, and that You are able to bring Your plan to pass in _____. My ways are not Your ways, and my thoughts are not Your thoughts. I thank you for thinking of my child and of me, and for doing things Your way in both of our lives. In the Name of Jesus! Amen.

Tuck the paper inside your Bible. When you sit down to spend time with God, get the paper out and thank God specifically for each aspect of this abundant life that you have asked for in faith.

CHAPTER TWENTY-ONE

Get Your Praise On

udden pain comes with an unexpected Friday phone call. Josh and Avaka have separated and it is all his fault. He wasn't ready to talk to me but she was.

Her cries on the phone skewered me. Rage. Hatred. Agony. I let her get it out. I felt somehow responsible, which is the first reaction of a recovering codependent. I should have raised him better. I failed. She cannot hear anything I'm saying about God getting her through this. I can't promise a happy ending only survival and a better life. Hearing her profanity and fury I see how lost she is, and yet who can blame her for this response? She knows no other way except the way of the world. Vengeance. After the initial venting I am the last person she wants to talk to right now because I don't hate my son and she wants me to.

My heart is so heavy and the tears don't stop and sleep doesn't come. Addicts, even in recovery, can inflict so much pain because their own inner hurt and anger spills out in an assortment of ways. *I need You, Lord.*

Flashback: Thirty six years ago my life was a shambles. I was living a double life, caught in a web of sin. Adultery, lying, drinking, pretense, self-love. *You were merciful to me to expose me, to stop me. You gave me a chance to start over.* I do understand there is a price we pay. Sowing and reaping, seedtime and harvest. It is the natural order of things either good or bad.

I must *get my praise on,* a phrase I learned at a church I once attended. Especially when I don't feel it. OK. Find something good in this horror. I praise God that he is alive, that his lies and addictions are beginning to surface, for this beautiful son, for the love he experienced from a good woman. *I need You, Lord.*

I cried a lot. I read Galatians. Freedom in Christ. Not just his. Mine. Is *unentangled* a word? No, but I want that. I kept my commitment to serve at church and while I was there received a text saying that Josh had called his brother-in-law Jim. First step out-up-forward. A friend called me and prayed and spoke encouragement and hope. A cloud as small as a man's fist is rising up on the horizon.

The weekend goes on. Church. Get in. Get out. Don't talk to anyone. The Holy Spirit is always working on my behalf. Joyce from church called Monday morning and asked what was wrong. I am more transparent than I intend. Through my tears I told her. I had been fasting and reading the Word and praying when she called. She understood. She hurt with me. And while she and I were on the phone, Josh called. I took the call, and while he and I talked she interceded in prayer. God you are so mighty. Who but You can orchestrate these details?

He and I cried together for an hour. Shame. Brokenness. Pieces of truth. Satan targets our weakness.

I thank God that in spite of all my missteps as a single parent, this child of mine still trusts me to love him when he is unlovable.

Can a mother forget her nursing child? Can she feel no love for the child she has borne?
But even if that were possible, I would not forget you!
See I have written your name on the palms of my hands.
Isaiah 49:15-16.

God has given mothers this ability to love that is so intertwined in the fabric of our soul that He compares His love for us to a mother's love. His is greater. But He gets mothers. He made us this way.

I cannot say this is all going to be okay because I don't know. But I know that which is hidden poisons the soul and this had to come out. As in the drug days, he got caught because God made sure of it. He is in the life changing business.

The next day I sought out a worship service. There is a place where praises are offered up to God in song for one day a week. It is a restful place. A sanctuary. A place where you can pray and find rest for your soul. Hardly anyone goes there. But I sought that place out the next day. Hour after hour I sat there soaking up the words to various worship songs and releasing pain.

May You be all that's on my mind
All of the time

Let my heart be torn into until Your will is mine.
Jesus.

I am in Your mind.
You reach out for me.

I don't want You to be a familiar stranger to me
Lord I want the fullness of knowing You in intimacy.

The Lord is the defense of my life.

You have no capacity to fail
You are Almighty God.

I can't understand this work of grace
How a perfect God could come and take my place.

I felt in my spirit that the pastor there had a word from God for me. Yet he left and I assumed that I was mistaken. Do I think I know how to hear from God? Apparently not, I thought. Suddenly this stranger, the pastor, was by my side. I poured it out. Just a few details. Immediately he called over two women. He said that God was doing a new thing during their Tuesday worship and intercession. People were standing in the gap for others who were not there. They were being anointed with oil in their place and miracles were happening. Like the Centurion who said *only say the word and my servant will be healed*, I am in need of a miracle right now. The anointing oil had a fragrance that nearly swept me into heaven. I wanted to stay there, wherever *there* was. I heard these words as I was anointed on behalf of Josh, Avaka, and Matthew: "Bondages are broken. Addictions are gone. Avaka is coming into the Kingdom. She will be a *force* in the Kingdom. The three of them could be serving God together in Europe. The anger will be gone in an instant, as quickly as it came. The love of God will so penetrate her heart that it will pour out of her everywhere she goes."

I stayed to praise, in total peace. This was the next song:

I sought the Lord and he heard my cry.
Tho sorrow may come in the night
Joy comes in the morning.

And just before I left after five hours of worshipping God, the very words that I had spoken to my son over the phone were sung out:

There is therefore no condemnation
For those who are in Christ Jesus.
Where are your accusers now?

I would love to say that the next five months were just one obvious miracle after another. Seedtime and harvest. Physical separation. Discouragement. Unforgiveness. Lonely holidays for Josh. Friends taking sides. Financial squeeze. Silent treatment. We could not rescue him from the price to be paid.

When doors were opened to speak by phone, I encouraged both Josh and Avaka separately. Josh made some wise choices. He showed up every night to take care of Matthew. He tried to find ways to show love, most of them nonverbal. Clean the house. Make her a dinner. Pay the bills even though you aren't living there. Eight hundred miles makes it easier for family to cope without knowing daily details. Some family members judge; most do not. All are sad about it and focus on finding reasons for joy as we gather together on Thanksgiving without dwelling on the pain we know he is feeling. None of us actually knew what she was feeling because she stopped communicating with us.

During this time I sent Avaka cards in the mail, texted scriptures telling of God's love for her, and sent small gifts. No response, but it's okay. I prayed that word that I heard about her. This built up my faith that it would come to pass, though it certainly didn't look like it.

I continued to do the things God set before me. I made my second trip to Haiti and taught a women's conference there called *Believing God.* As I teach others I teach myself. With his permission, I used Josh's story of addiction and deliverance during the conference. I always do and it always stirs hearts. All over the world there are mothers and fathers who are suffering with the choices their beloved children have made. His story fills those parents with hope. Believe God. I spared them the details of the latest disappointment, but it was because I really believed that all would be well. I was seeing them in my mind's eye back together. See the fist-sized cloud coming over the horizon.

Without fanfare sometime during the fifth month, Josh moved back to his home.

Almost without exception men keep a lot in. We didn't get the details; we never expect to. Don't need them.

God is bringing to pass His promise for an abundant life. Healing, marriage, children, career, ministry. It was not one child but two. With head-spinning speed Avaka became pregnant with their second son. I was there in their home when the pregnancy test revealed two pink lines. They didn't have those in my day. That means *pregnant.* Clearly both were happy about it and said so. They are going to church together every Sunday. They are buying a second home as an investment. This looks like commitment. Josh's Facebook posts are the two of them or the three of them together with this phrase borrowed from the coffee shop he works at: *Loving Life.*

It's a journey. A walk of faith. My prayer over my son now is based on I Timothy 3:1-4 *"I pray that Josh will desire for an honorable position in the Kingdom and in a local church. May he be a man above reproach, faithful to Avaka. May he exercise self-control, live wisely, and have a good reputation. May he enjoy having guests in his home, and be able to teach. He will not be a heavy drinker or be violent. he will be gentle, not quarrelsome, and not a lover of money. He will manage his own family well, having children who love and respect him. He will manage his own household well so that he can also take care of God's church."*

Women could be deacons in New Testament churches, and the same standards apply to them.

God knows His intentions toward my son. But praying His personalized word helps me to keep my own eyes on what I cannot yet see.

Seek First to Understand

1. Would anything you could have done prevented the latest relapse or stray into sin? __ __ (Hint: The correct answer has only two letters.)

2. *Create in me a clean heart, O God; Renew a right spirit within me.* According to Psalm 51:10, whose heart does God hold you accountable for?

3. Recall a scripture or lesson you may have learned during the early stages of your child's addiction behavior. How does that reapply in this latest situation?

God's Word

I pray that from his glorious, unlimited resources he will empower you with inner strength through his Spirit. Then Christ will make his home in your heart as you trust in him. Your roots will grow down into God's love and keep you strong. And may he have the power to understand, as all God's people should, how wide, how long, how high, and how deep his love is. May he experience the love of Christ...Then he will be made complete with all the fullness of life and power that comes from God. Ephesians 3:16-19

Prayer

Lord, thank you for patience and mercy toward me during all those years of my own rebellion and ignorance of your ways. When I am disappointed or angry again, help me to remember how very many times I failed to do what I knew was right in your eyes. Let me recall your loving promise that I no longer walk in condemnation. I am made new. And what you have done for me you will do for my children. I am grateful, Father, for your unfailing love toward me, and I extend that now to my child. In Jesus. Amen.

CHAPTER TWENTY-TWO

Aslan is on the Move

Two years pass. Their lives look Facebook perfect. But I know they really aren't. Poor communication. Secrecy. Separate bank accounts. Two houses. A beautiful second son. Strong business. Going to church most Sundays. Bragging rights. He's great. The poster child of kicking that bastard heroin.

I was to have been in Haiti with my son just last week. My dream was coming true...our first mission trip together. He said he couldn't get away from work and kept trying to back out. He told me not to buy his ticket but I bought it anyway because I was just so confident of each step of God's plan for both of us. Suddenly I got really sick with anemia and exhaustion. My body wouldn't retain iron or make new red blood cells. Then poly-neuropathy surfaced in both feet. I wasn't sleeping and could hardly walk from the shooting pain up my legs. I was so disappointed. Where was my quick healing? I cancelled the trip. While the rest of the mission team was doing what I wanted to do, my daughter was caring for me at her home. Why, God??

Lying prone on the sofa of my daughter's home I received the first call from Avaka asking me if I knew what was going on with Josh. I did not know anything, but I had noticed him being edgy on Facetime calls. Facetime makes it harder to hide truth. He looked terrible. Haggard. Obvious weight loss. When I asked him about it he attributed it to working long hours and not eating or sleeping well. He was looking away, not making eye contact. I dismissed heroin as a possibility because he was working long hours every day in his print shop and twelve years ago he was always tired and barely able to function. I assured Avaka it couldn't be that. Days passed. Finally he called me and told me he was using prescription drugs, amphetamines. Avaka went with him to the doctor. The doctor put him on a drug to bring him down. In a matter of a few days his Facebook-perfect world is crumbling.

Day 0. Old Testament prophets Zechariah and Ezekiel both referred to *the day of the Lord* or *that day* as the moment the Israelites recognized Jesus as their rejected Savior. Truth is known. No excuses accepted. Grief and sorrow prevail. On *that day* for our family Avaka Facetimed me from their car sitting on the parking lot of a favorite ice cream shop. Josh and Matthew were at the window ordering. She said she found a burned spoon and needles in his toiletries bag. I calmly responded, *that is heroin*. I don't think I'll ever forget the look of agony on her face as this truth sunk in. Pure fear. My emergency adrenaline kicked in. Cope. Don't fall apart. We talked briefly about what to do next. I encouraged her to deal with it today. Confront today. He was coming back to the car. She had to get off the phone.

Boom! The calls started coming. First Avaka, then Josh, then Avaka, then convo with his dad, then sisters, then Avaka, then Josh, then Avaka. Immediately I understood what I had resented. My son was in deep trouble again and I didn't know. No wonder Josh didn't want to go to Haiti. How could he? Where would he shoot up? God had wanted me here to take the calls, to intercede, to alert the prayer people, to save his life again. I would not have wanted to be anywhere else but on my daughter's sofa.

What was in the dark is coming into the light. All trust is gone in the marriage. Children were put at risk. Financial wreckage. Lies upon lies. Later that night he called me crying, sobbing, reaching out to me but still using. I am OK with hard truth, but then realize I wasn't even getting the hard truth but more lies. He had been going high to *Celebrate Recovery*. Going high to Sunday church with family. Trying to keep living his life with methadone from the doctor...but Googling how to use both methadone and heroin without being found out. Deception of others but worst of all deception of self. Begging for one more chance to do this without inpatient rehab. Avaka insists that I come. I can't. I am barely walking. I am where God wants me...flat on my back in another city. I will not be the *watcher* of my son to keep him clean. Won't work. I'm trying to let it be her decision but that's not helpful to her. Avaka and I are close to agreeing to *one more chance* and once again I am at risk of getting sucked into his web of deception and the ticking time bomb. I am acting calm but really I am numb from my neuropathic feet up.

The pathway to taking up your cross is bloody and excruciating and many others who love you run scared or stumble along battered and bleeding beside you.

Twelve years clean. **Relapse.**

Small but deadly word. Like a bullet to the gut.

Opioids and heroin.

Prince just died of this.

But God.

Intervenes.

Day 1: Andrea and Jim weigh in. No option. All of us have been here before. All of us made mistakes. Learn. Jim loves this brother but is further removed from the gene pool and more objective. Andrea acts as his mouthpiece. It must happen now, not two days from now. He could die in that two days. Heroin is sometimes laced with fentanyl. It instantly kills. I listen. Avaka listens. I am awake most of the night. Prayer.

4:00 am I received this text from Andrea: *The warriors are praying. Aslan is on the move.* I fell asleep.

The Elders at Believers Church in Tulsa are up praying in early morning for my boy. My family and a few prayer warriors who love him are praying for this man who is still my boy. Let him make the right decision.

Grandma Wilma places her hand on a picture of Jim's prayer room in his office and speaks deliverance from addiction for my son.

I've been studying the spiritual armor of God. Put it on. Jesus is in every piece.

I read about Elisha. Open your eyes. See. The Lord's Armies are gathered. No need to fear. No one can stand against them.

Day 2. A strong wife, a good friend, and a surrogate local mom all confront and demand. He argues. He refuses. He falls into the mom's arms and sobs. Finally he yields. He will go to rehab. Another good friend agrees to drive in from North Carolina to run his business while he gets help. He is loved. Avaka's best friend is there from Slovakia so she is not alone. God knew and orchestrated these details.

Waiting. Waiting. Hours pass. I hear nothing. At the end of the day I get a text. He is safe. Checked in. Breathe. Rest.

Money will be needed from me for rehab. OK. I will make a loan to be repaid by him. Learn from the past. Owning the responsibility and restitution is critical for recovery.

An angry phone call with his father, my ex-husband, jerks me right back into the weakness and fear of my past. I had held it together. But this is the straw. I cry. Both parents have quickly resorted to our old behaviors.

Exhausted sleep. Awake two hours. Read John 10 and Psalm 91. Jesus is the door, the gate. He guards His sheep. We know His voice. 850 miles removed from his pain. Didn't have to see him say goodbye to his sons. I listen to *It Is Well With My Soul.* It's going to be okay.

Day 3. Time alone. Don't think about it. I tell one friend what's happening and she says *write the book*. I prayed with another friend on the phone. Encouraged for the moment. Where are my usual emotions? There have been few tears. I am mostly calm. It might be because this is a new experience. His wife is making the decisions. It is her place. Easier when it's not me. And also because I've been here before and I've learned. I trust God to use this to bring him to wholeness for the first time in his life. Real, true, unabashed love for God. It's time for him to carry his cross. I am stronger now than I was twelve years ago. And I've seen God work. I know there is a vision not yet accomplished in either Josh's or Avaka's lives and something drastic needed to happen to get them on that path. When the daily calls stop and I don't know what's happening, the battle for my peace ramps up. Fight fear. Don't let the adversary get what he wants.

Day 4. Remnants of Day 3. Awake most of the night. Pray in the Spirit. Read John 10 again. No one will snatch one of the sheep given to Jesus out of God's hand. *He belongs to you, Lord. I know he does.* His spirit is safe. I read online about the addiction center where he is tonight. Mixed reviews. Doctor uses pharmacological intervention (methodone) as well as 12 steps, counseling, aftercare. So he will come out of there in 30 days hooked on methodone. They will suggest he stay for another $25K worth of cure. His wife wants to send him away for a year. That saddens and frightens me. Hence, the lack of sleep. Wide awake at 2:30 a.m., I read online about heroin addiction, the physiological craving for dopamine in his brain. His utter helplessness to stop himself from getting the next fix. But that is a lie and I have prayed for truth. The truth is that Jesus, the Truth, the Way, and the Life, is THE Healer. Dr. Caroline Leaf, a brain scientist and Christian, says you can change your brain. When the Spirit of Christ comes, helping you to seek the Lord and examine the lies you have believed and replace them with truth, your brain literally begins to change. I know from my life that when you get Christ-centered, the excitement He gives you is a high like no other. Teaching the Word and ministering to others fulfills better than booze or drugs or sex. My addictions were to men and sex. But it never lasted. On the day I truly repented and said *"I need Jesus!"* in desperation, that change was instant. That desire went away. There was anger and unforgiveness to peel away and that would have to come, too. As long as I kept my focus on the greater purpose for my life, I could live a pure life no matter what others around me chose. God's word is true. There is NO THING He cannot conquer. I must believe and believe and believe that.

Does this writing sound scattered? I read it over. Yes, it does because that's how my emotions run when he's using and lying and stealing. I should be handling this better. Peaceful, calm...then not. Confident, hopeful...then not. And yours? Great mother or father of faith, on those days when the bullet of relapse hits you in the gut, how do you respond? If you never wavered in faith you wouldn't be reading this book. If this reminds you of yourself and the irregular rhythm of your heart on *that day* then you are not alone. It is a fight of faith because our adversary wants to destroy us as well as our child. Perhaps our health, perhaps our stability, but most certainly our faith and focus on doing the works God prepared in advance for us to do. I must begin to talk and plan for my own life even while I get through this *time of evil*.

My daughter texts: *For today he is safe.*

I am short-cutting to *get well fast* mode. There will be many calls and many decisions made, mostly by other people. And while Josh and Avaka and the boys will be always *there* in my thoughts, God wants me to live my life. I will plan another trip to Haiti without Josh. I will lead my Wednesday *Coffee with God* group. I will lead middle-school youth once a month and love them. I will embrace and enjoy every moment with my grandchildren in all three states. I will be best friends with my daughters every day. Sometimes I will bring children who are strangers into my home and protect them for a few days while their own mamas are in crisis. I will respond to the people God presents to me with an invitation to encourage, to love, and in some cases to guide to Jesus. I will live my life, the one God prepared for me. And I will finish this book with whatever ending God provides.

Seek First to Understand

1. If you have been through a relapse, a slip back into hell, what emotions or behaviors showed up immediately? Examples might be anxiety, loss of appetite, sickness, sleeplessness, tension, anger. Complete this sentence in writing: I feel _____ I am experiencing _____

   _____

   _____

2. There are only two emotions, love and fear. All descriptors and symptoms stem from one or the other. What or who is the source of fear?   John 10:10.

3. Try to identify exactly what you fear. Next to each descriptor or symptom write one or two words elaborating on what you fear. For example, if you are sleepless, perhaps you fear *not knowing* or *no control* when you are asleep. If you are angry, perhaps you fear *a particular person (name)* or *being wounded.*

4. Who is the source of love?

5. Find a scripture to combat each one of those lies. Cross out the lie and write the truth according to God next to it. For example, for sleepless you might write *Proverbs 3:24 You can go to bed without fear; you will lie down and sleep soundly.* For no control you might write *2 Timothy 1:7 For God didn't give me a spirit of fear, but a spirit of love, power and self-control.*

6. Revisit this list of emotions for a few days. Think about how much you have grown in this area since first beginning to deal with your fears. Thank God that He is using this to make you more Christlike.

God's Word

*If we confess our sins to him, he is faithful to forgive us our sins
and to cleanse us from all unrighteousness.*
I John 1:9

*You, however, know all about my teaching, my way of life,
my purpose, faith, patience, love, endurance, persecutions, sufferings
- what kind of things happened to me in Antioch, Iconium, and Lysra,
the persecutions I endured.
Yet the Lord rescued me from all of them.*
2 Timothy 3:10

And the woman received her dead back to life.
Hebrews 11:35

Prayer

Lord, thank you once again for saving my child's life. My heart is filled with gratitude. Thank you that you do not give up on my child or on me. You have been patient and filled with lovingkindness toward us. I place the armor on each of us. The belt of truth is on our waists. We will not lie or believe a lie. The breastplate of righteousness is on our chests. Our hearts are guarded from any fatal blow. We will live and not die. The Gospel of Peace is on our feet. We are prepared to go anywhere you send us and bring peace into the situation with us. I place the helmet of salvation on our heads. We have the mind of Christ. Our thinking is guarded. We are new creations in Christ and that old toxic cloud in our brains is gone. We lift up the shield of faith - trusting you to rescue us from every attack. We pick up the sword of God's word, the most powerful weapon with which we fight. I am asking for my child's healing - spiritual, emotional, and physical. I ask for a new marriage - far better than the one they have had. I thank you for protecting their children. You are good, Lord. We will praise you no matter what. You have given us the power, love, and self-control of the Spirit of God. Hold our hands while we walk down this path once again. In Christ, Amen.

CHAPTER TWENTY-THREE

Day Five

onversation with Avaka lasted less than ten minutes and yet filled me with hope. This is a woman who had no experience with drugs or drug culture. Nothing in her European, Catholic, hard-working, independent background prepared her for this. She married a young man with secrets. She didn't know about his heroin addiction or Hepatitis C. He deceived her. She has had every *right* to hold him in contempt.

The "F" bomb gets dropped as that anger surfaces in our conversation. I do not respond.

Five and one half years ago they took off for Las Vegas and had a chapel wedding without family. He looked young and innocent and scared. She looked sophisticated, beautiful, stately. He was clean, sober, sweet and kind. She was naive and totally trusting. Our family was hurt not to be at the secret wedding. There was mistrust. Why did she marry him? Citizenship? Not really. She didn't care to be a U.S citizen. She did need legal status and she did love this young man. But she didn't expect to be with him forever. This marriage was for a time.

I decided to love her. In good times we have laughed together. We have shared family history. But I did not share about the drugs or the Hep C. I wanted her to know but I was scared for her to know. And it wasn't my place to tell her. In five plus years my family has grown to really love her. There is laughter. There is cooking and baking together. There are babies to hold and kid stories to share. There is friendship with her mother.

In the last four days she has been courage, strength, wisdom. How, Lord? Only by You and yet I don't know her real heart toward you. Only You know that. But somehow, some way, you have moved through her to save her husband's life.

It was Avaka who confronted, who would not back down, who protected her children, who gave her credit card at the Destin Addiction Recovery Center and left her husband there.

It was Avaka who searched his cell phone for drug dealer phone numbers, who saw the extent of his credit card debt with most of his resources gone. Savings gone. Business reserves depleted.

The adversary comes to steal. I withdrew money from my 401K and sent it to her. I have sent money for immediate help from my savings. She expressed her gratitude.

There is not enough money to pay bills...business, household or otherwise. Her salary as an accountant will not cover all the household bills. Help will be needed and it must come from his family. She is a hard worker and a saver who always has money. But the burden of hospital bills and childcare has been all on her, and her own reserves are gone.

Fear can both speak and be silenced.

Today I hear these amazing things from her. She is willing to quit the job she loves, sell his business, sell their homes, and relocate *with him* to a place where he can get help and start over. She wants the man she married. She wants the father of her children to live. She will commit to one year of trying. She will try her very hardest to save his life and their marriage and his fatherhood. She says he needs God.

This is love.

Two years ago when they were separated and I was sitting heartbroken in Destiny Church worshipping God, the pastor spoke this word over her:

Avaka will come into the Kingdom. Her anger will leave as quickly as it came. She will be a force in the Kingdom. She and Josh will probably minister together in Europe.

I believed it though I couldn't see how that would happen. That's what faith is. *Now* Faith is believing *now* for what will happen in the future even though you can't see the steps to getting there.

I would never have chosen this step. God didn't choose for him to shoot heroin into his veins again. God caused him to get caught so he had to stop. God saved his life. God gave him this wife five years ago.

The unknown of what happens at the end of 28 days looms large. But for today, the willingness of this young woman to choose love and commitment stills my heart and inspires me.

Aslan is on the move.

Seek First to Understand

1. God had told Abram that he would make him into a great nation. That meant children. Yet God gave him Sarai, a beautiful yet barren woman, for his wife. She left everything to go with Abram. But a severe famine happened and they had to go Egypt to survive. There she lied for him. Not only was his life spared but he gained riches because of her. They left there with a slave girl named Hagar who created a boatload of problems down the road. You can read this account in Genesis 12 and 16.

2. Who else besides you loves your child? Could God be using him in their lives or them in his life to accomplish far greater than what you have been willing to see? What greater purpose? What good qualities does God see?

God's Word

Trust steadily in God, hope unswervingly, love extravagantly.
And the best of the three is love.
1 Corinthians 13:13b (Message)

I give them eternal life, and they will never perish.
No one can snatch them away from me.
John 10:28

And we know that God causes everything to work together for the good of those who
love God and are called according to His purpose for them.
Romans 8:28

Prayer

Lord, I thank you for your love for me and for my child. Thank you for every person who loves us. Give me wisdom to deal with the people I don't understand. Help me to love them as you love them and trust the details of these complex relationships to you. Help me get myself out of the way of your purposes so that the good you want to do is accomplished.

CHAPTER TWENTY-FOUR

Walk Down Memory Lane

*D*ay 6. I checked out mentally for a couple of days. I knew he
was in a safe place. I just stopped talking about it or dwelling on
it. My mind needed a rest. I spent two days in the downstairs playroom
transferring old family VHS tapes onto DVDs. That required that I watch
them all. This was my private therapy session.

Josh at seven dancing to *Can't Touch This* at our 25th anniversary party
until we just had to stop him because there was no end to it.

Sitting next to me while I opened his birthday gifts to me. His hand was in
my hair. Kisses on cheeks.

Christmases with mounds of gifts that I hoped would ease the pain of no
dad in the house. Aunts and Uncles and Grandpa Bell and Granny Alice
loving on him. Josh wearing a huge sweatshirt that said *World's Best*

Grandma two Christmas mornings in a row. It was a gift she received on her last Christmas on earth. It was his way of remembering her. This is the heart of the boy.

Pinewood Derby. Last place car because his reluctant Den Mother (me) helped him rather than someone with tool skill.

Jumping and dancing on a trampoline with the water sprinkler at full blast underneath, the slipperiest surface imaginable. What was I thinking?

His tenth birthday party with a rented chimpanzee and his handler in our backyard with a gaggle of boys. He was for sure the most popular boy in the world on that day.

The girls. Concert choir. Show choir. Leah dancing like a princess. First place trophies for Winterguard. Weekend trips to marching band competitions. He was always there. Watching. Cheering. Family.

Andrea's wedding. She was stunning and so very happy. Josh was a groomsman. All was well with the world.

We morphed into teenage years. The Christmas beagle, Spanky. Mouth kisses from Josh to Spanky. The Easter Egg Hunt with $$$ inside. Andrea and Jim newlyweds, Leah in college, Josh at 13-14. Racing through the house to get the eggs. Laughter. Competition. More laughter. Josh locking them out. Pure fun.

Then my hands found the DVD marked *Josh*. I put it in the player. I had not seen this. He was in his bedroom with two electric guitars and his drum set. His brown hair was bleached blonde. He had recorded himself playing songs he had written. As soon as he opened his mouth the *F-bombs* started flowing out. It felt dark. He put himself down. More *F-bombs*. I couldn't watch it all and didn't include it with the family memories I transferred to DVDs. But it was a noticeable difference. He was 15 or 16 by then. There was anger. A marked change in personality. Gone was the smiling family boy. In his place was this morose brooding teenager playing loud music that didn't sound like music to these ears.

Yes, that was sad and it was the beginning of the drug years, the angry boy who had to go live with his dad because his behavior was more than I could handle.

But overall, when I reflected on what was on twenty years of videos I saw a family well provided for. I heard laughter. I saw love. He was given a good life. We all were. I bought that video camera after their dad moved out, so the daily tension of alcoholism wasn't in the picture. Mothers always struggle with guilt and self-blame that we just didn't do it all right and there was no dad and perhaps if I had tried harder or read parenting books or hadn't ever dated anyone or went to the perfect church or ....

My private therapy session with a box of old VHS tapes was a gift to help me remember the sweet happy child that is still inside my son. The whole family includes beautiful daughters enjoying life and graduating and marrying, and the good things, the very very good things we have had and still have. God orchestrates a submitted life. He provided the means for me to provide a good home for my family. We never lacked for anything we truly needed. He is weaving the tapestry together. I needed to look at the fine stitches on the back to see His craftsmanship in our lives and to understand that a complete and beautiful picture is emerging for the world to see.

After my two-day vacation from *this present darkness,* I emerge and will re-engage in family discussions about *the problem.* I have not prayed much these days, if at all. Yet I felt the Presence of God with me. It was as if He was saying *See the love. Remember the good.*

Seek First to Understand

Your best therapy can be in a rocking chair on the front porch in a rainstorm. It might look like mine did, a walk down memory lane through photo journals or the volume of pics stored on your many devices. Think deeply about the happy family times and how the Lord developed each of your childrens' lives. See the good mother in those remembrances. Perspective. Big picture. God's story ends well. So does yours.

God's Word

Give thanks to the Lord, for he is good. His faithful love endures forever.
Psalm 118:29

He took some bread and gave thanks to God for it.
Then He broke it into pieces and gave it to the disciples saying,
"This is my body which is given for you. Do this in remembrance of me.
Luke 22:19

Take communion. You can do this at home. A piece of cracker and a small drink of grape juice. Thanksgiving. *1 Corinthians 11:23-28*

Prayer

Father, thank you for the unexpected ways you help me to see the big picture of Your presence. In the painful valleys You always give us a place to reflect on the truth of who we are. You know my errors, but You still say I am good and my children are good because You made us.

CHAPTER TWENTY FIVE

Day Ten

This is not all falling into place. Avaka and Josh's conference call did not go well. She reports to me that he was profane, argumentative and totally self-focused. He wants to leave the treatment center today. He sends word through her that no family member is to pay for his treatment because he's not staying. She is panicked when she calls me. What will she do if he walks out? If he comes home? She is frightened. I remain calm in my voice if not my emotions. I counsel her: *You will be strong. You will not back down. No one can keep him there against his will, but he cannot come home. He will not be allowed to be with his sons. Hang on.* He expressed no concern for her and she is disappointed, of course.

Avaka called me to report this just as my niece and her family arrived at the front door. Do I put on a happy face? No. I'm tired of that. No more pretense. I waited until after lunch and then told them that my son was in a treatment center and might not stay. There was no sense of judgment, only sadness. At some point in our lives we have all faced our own imperfections and we find that grace is our friend. We immediately prayed together holding hands. No family secrets this go-round. Neither will juicy details be shared. Just the facts among the praying people. That's all they need.

Andrea, our family counselor in training and practice, upon considering that her brother might walk out of recovery that night, gave strong advice to Avaka about money. Close all joint accounts so he has no access to money. He is not trustworthy right now. It's the sickness. To help a drug addict you must do what you can to cut off his access to money. Drugs and money are codependent. Avaka is not materialistic, yet she is very security-conscious. She confesses her pain in finding that he has stolen cash from her tip stash from her part time job as a server. There is understandable anger. Will she ever be able to trust him at all about anything? Andrea gives her hope. Yes, it can be restored but they will need intensive marriage counseling later. Not yet, not until he's sane again. Using drugs or alcohol when you have proven to yourself over and over that it robs you of all that is good in your life is insane. Andrea is crying herself to sleep because she knows it's the right counsel to give but it feels like a betrayal of her brother. She loves him so much. The pain of addiction spreads like a fungus on the branches of the tree.

This is his fourth time in rehab. Twice in short term like this. Once long-term, a 12 month mandatory stay. Now this. Realistically he's where I would expect him to be after ten days. He's barely detoxed from the worst of the poison in his body but it's still speaking. Does anyone really go into treatment because they wake up one day and decide they are out of control? *No!* Everyone is there because there were no options. The money had run out, the lies had been found out, and they were given no options by someone who loved them and had not yet given up on them.

Of course he is still thinking that he's got this under control. He can do this. So the problem is not him but these people who love him, who don't trust him to live in the same neighborhood, to go to his business where dealers deliver his drugs and handle the same daily pressures of work, marriage, and parenting but this time do it all perfectly and without falling.

Dear sweet Leah. Her focus is on taking care of me. She put the boys to bed and then came down and laid across the bed so I could just spill out some emotions. She has stocked the small frig in my room with fresh fruit, Gatorade, bottled water and Dove chocolates. Acts of love and kindness are keeping me going.

Alone again. Sleep evades. I get a late night call from Andrea. *Thanksgiving precedes miracles,* she tells me. *For today, he is alive.* She is thanking God that Josh will be an evangelist in this lifetime. He will tell others about Jesus. That doesn't mean he will be paid to do that. He could tell his print shop customers. He could tell it over coffee with a friend. We are all called to draw people to God. *We believe, therefore we speak.* First we must believe it and hold onto that belief. Why not him? There are many testimonies of people who came out of drug addiction to set the world on fire for Jesus. Why not Josh? I thank God before I toss and turn into sleep that He is the creator of intervention. He is doing one right now in my son's life. How grateful I am for that lifeline just before I close my eyes, emotionally and physically spent.

That night I awoke at 3 am. The report of the phone call must have been coursing through my short-term memory, while I choose to let it take root or boot it out. Josh's words right now are not his. Heroin is talking. We fight not against flesh and blood but against spiritual forces and authorities. I am awake. I'm fighting. I spoke back with authority. *"In the Name of Jesus, I command heroin to be silenced! You may not speak through my son again!"*

Alone in the downstairs bedroom at my daughter's house I pray in the Spirit and in English, and I silence the spirits that come from the belly of the beast. I release the power of heaven onto my son. I say the Lord's Prayer. Where is God? He is over all, honored, total power, total love. He is our Father. Mine, Josh's, Avaka's, Andrea's, Leah's, James, all of ours. All of us are under his watchful care. He is in Heaven. He sees all that is happening. *Thy Kingdom come.* We have a Kingdom viewpoint. We pray for his Kingdom solutions. *Jesus come into this situation. Thy will be done.* His process; not ours. That our wills are submitted to His. He is working His plan for Josh's and Avaka's lives.

On earth as it is in Heaven. God gave us authority on the earth so we have to take it and use it on the earth just as He uses it in Heaven. The s*poken* word of God - He spoke and the world was created. We must speak. *Give us this day our daily bread.* Not yesterday's mistakes or tomorrow's fears and unknowns, but grace to live this day and make decisions this day. The Bread of Life...Jesus. Let us partake.

Lead us not into temptation. The temptation is to be deceived, to control, to fear and worry. The temptation for Josh to manipulate so that the craving of his physical body can be satisfied until it destroys him. Don't let us go there, Lord. Not Josh, not Avaka, not me, not Andrea, not James *but deliver us from evil.* The adversary has a plot to destroy each and all of us; this family.

Our Deliverer Jesus is here and now. We are delivered. Let us rest in His refuge and continuously call on His name. Jesus Jesus Jesus. *For*

Thine is the Kingdom, the power, and the glory forever. Amen. The end of all things is God. This is His Kingdom that we rest in. He has all power to rescue us. It is for His glory that we will be rescued.

I searched the scriptures for my underlined passages, those that I have prayed over him and myself so many times before. Lamentations 3:25 jumps out. *Great is His faithfulness. His mercies begin afresh each morning.* These words I meditate on silently. *The Lord is my inheritance therefore I will hope in Him.* How many times God has proved himself faithful. It is important what I say to myself. Today is a new day.

After a few hours sleep I am awake. Check phone. Discard junk emails. Leave the Christian ones. Maybe read later. Maybe not. But there's one from Joseph Prince, the pastor from Singapore whose cable program has often lulled me back to sleep with the word of God on sleepless nights in St. Louis. Today's email blast is perfect: The Prodigal. *The father gave him sandals as soon as he returned. Servants don't get sandals, only children get them,* says Pastor Prince. The shoes. The Good News. Josh is a child of God. He has shoes on. He knows the Good News. His feet are *shod*, those shoes are nailed on there permanently. I must meditate on that, remembering who he is today. That little boy all innocence and laughter and kisses is buried beneath 25 years of burden for now. *But he IS a child of God, the Most High God, the Almighty Father, and that shall not be taken from him.*

Seek First to Understand

1. What wakes you up at night? Journal any dreams you are having, thoughts, or people that occupy your mind just as you wake up.

2. What might God be trying to show you about your fears or people in your life?

3. God wants to give you understanding. Ask Him for it.

4. Pray for the living people you dreamed about. What lies might you be believing that need to be replaced by a truth from God's word.

5. What spirit might be speaking through the people in your night thoughts?

6. Speak with the authority you have been given and command that spirit to shut up!

God's Word

When he came to his senses, he said, 'How many of my father's hired men
have food to spare, and here I am starving to death.'
Luke 15:17

But the father said to his servants, 'Quick! Bring the best robe and put it on him.
Put a ring on his finger and sandals on his feet.'
Luke 15:22

Finally, be strong in the Lord and in his mighty power.
Put on the full armor of God so that you can take your stand
against the devil's schemes. For our struggle is not against flesh and blood,
but against the rulers, against the authorities, against the powers of this dark world
and against the spiritual forces of evil in the heavenly realms.
Ephesians 6:10-11

Stand firm, then, with the belt of truth buckled around your waist,
with the breastplate of righteousness in place,
and with your feet fitted with the readiness that comes from the gospel of peace.
Ephesians 6:15

Prayer

Lord, thank you for the gift of the Holy Spirit in me. With His power in me I can take my stand against the schemes and attacks against me and my family. I win. Your love sustains me and your faithfulness gives me hope. You speak through the people around me to encourage me. I wake up each day knowing that this is a new day and you are still at work. Give us all understanding. Help us to come to our senses, to recognize the lies we have believed and replace them with truth. Thank you for the peace of God that reigns over each family member. We walk in the Good News even when we aren't conscious of it. We think peace, speak peace, and take it with us everywhere we go. Guard our minds from fear. In the Name and Power of Jesus Christ. Amen.

CHAPTER TWENTY SIX

A Certain Kind of Peace

Battles are fought on multiple fronts. The enemy we are fighting will always try to box you in and divide your attention. He has a much better chance of winning if your attention is drawn away from his weakest point. I had been battling an immune system disorder that had caused anemia and polyneuropathy. Extreme fatigue and foot and leg pain had come on suddenly and resulted in me staying with my daughter Leah for an entire month. I proudly and frequently announced that I was very independent and quite capable of taking care of myself. Until I wasn't. Reluctantly I was using a walker and being driven to doctor's appointments and dropped off at the door. A handicapped parking pass...cool.

Dealing with relapse could have waited until I was well, couldn't it, God?

I found myself staying away from church. I had my excuses: it was too hard for me to stand that long and it would be impossible for Leah to get me to my own church because hers started at the same time. Truth: I could have gotten there had I wanted. And no one would have minded if I sat the whole time. I didn't want to be there because I did not want to walk into a smiling, hand-shaking, shoulder-hug-greeting of six people sitting near me like my world is fine, like their world is fine because it isn't and theirs probably isn't either. That felt like religion and I needed the grace that flows from the body of Christ. That need was being met by the Wednesday coffee ladies.

My Wednesday ladies. Small group, cell group, home group, whatever they call it in churches that encourage believers to meet together in small gatherings weekly. Six months ago I was ready to stop meeting. It had been a year and I thought I needed a break as the leader. No one wanted to stop so I reluctantly agreed to keep going. God alone knew how much I would need this circle of friends during my own crisis. I had walked away from church in the early years of my marriage. When the marriage turned dark and sour I had no one I could trust with the truth. I did have a couple of good Christian friends when I went through this with Josh at 14, at 15, 16, 17, 18, 19, and 20. They prayed for me and spoke encouraging words on my down days. But a couple of church changes and lost connections could have found me without support. Ah, the Wednesday coffee. We knew a lot about each other and it all stayed in our circle. Not once has anything surfaced that was shared outside this group. We don't have to be with people who have gone through exactly the same things. However, in our world today we find that most people in a group, even a wonderful churchgoing Christian group, have been touched by addiction in their families. They don't ask details. They let me cry and hold me if I need it. They took turns picking me up and driving me to meetings. God threw me another lifeline.

Finally I was back in my home. I found myself with a certain urgency to get up and get moving because there were other important things going on. Life was still happening. Good intentions aside, I spent the first day on the sofa all afternoon...thinking about things, praying, napping. Then I turned on a message from Believers Church in Tulsa. *Strength in Weakness* 2 Corinthians 12.

We are strong only when our weakness forces us to admit that we are powerless unless Jesus does something. It is Step One of addiction recovery. And I am there. I am no longer the mother of a rebellious teenager that I am legally responsible for. I am in the back seat of the car with an adult son and only occasionally invited to speak. I can't force Josh to stay in a treatment center if he chooses to walk out. I can't make Avaka take him back home, nor would I want to. I can't make him come to Jesus and get well. I can't make him stay away from a drug dealer who's got his number and address.

In that admission of my helplessness, there is a certain kind of peace that settles in. The responsibility for what happens is actually resting on Jesus. He is working in my son's life in the way he knows is best to accomplish a healing that is deeper than I can fathom. I will believe in that. I will believe in Him. He loves me. He loves my son. He wants to carry my burden. I give it to him.

For the next two mornings I listened to praise music first thing. I haven't done that for awhile. I am not anxious. I am at rest.

Seek First to Understand

1. Step one from <u>A Spiritual Journey</u>: We admitted we were powerless over the effects of our separation from God---that our lives had become unmanageable. *I know nothing good lives in me, that is, in my sinful nature. For I have the desire to do what is good, but I cannot carry it out. Romans 7:18*

2. Do you find yourself making excuses for staying away from church? If so, why?

3. Write on this line or in your journal the times when your life has been better when you kept your distance from God and Christians who walk in grace._____

4. Who is in charge of your child's life right now? Of yours?

God's Word

We now have this light shining in our hearts.
We ourselves are like fragile clay jars containing this great treasure.
This makes it clear that our great power is from God and not ourselves.
2 Corinthians 4:7

Prayer
from Psalm 40:2-3

Lord, thank you for lifting my child and me out of the muck and the mire. Thank you for setting our feet on solid ground and steadying us as we walk along. Thank you for giving us a new song to sing, a hymn of praise to our God. Many will see what You have done in my life and my child's life and be amazed. They will put their trust in the Lord. In Christ. Amen.

THE LION, THE WITCH, AND THE WARDROBE
C. S. Lewis

And Aslan, not at all slacking his pace, rushed straight as a bullet toward it.

"The Witch's home!" he cried. "Now, children, hold tight."

CHAPTER TWENTY SEVEN

Codependency No More

Three letters from the Recovery Center

#1: *I'm officially opiate free today. I'm feeling really crappy. Sweats and chills and sleepless nights. I can't believe I went down this path again and am filled with shame. I cry pretty much every afternoon when I'm alone. 32 years old and I'm in rehab again. I'm so fearful that something is going to happen to the boys while I'm in here and I'll blame myself forever. It's irrational but it's there. I pray and it helps a little. I know you paid money so I could stay longer. Thanks for that. I'm really trying to get better once and for all. I want to be a better husband and father desperately. They all deserve it. Anyways, tell everyone hello and I'm doing okay. Love you, Josh*

#2: *Hope you're well. I'm bummed I'll be unable to call you this Sunday (Mother's Day) but I promise I'll be thinking about you and Avaka. I'm feeling much better these days. Physically I'm 100%. I'm fully detoxed and feeling like myself. I'm also not so emotional anymore. Spiritually I'm getting back into a good routine of praying, which hasn't happened in a long time. I'm feeling optimistic about the future.*

After lots of prayer and surrender I know the boys will be safe and protected while I'm in here. ... I still don't want to be here, but I'm trying to surrender to the process. The real change is going to happen by working the steps and going to meetings, both of which I'm willing to do. I'm going to ask my counselor about transferring to intensive outpatient for my final 7 days. Basically I still attend the AA meetings, classes, counseling sessions, drug tests but I sleep at home and have a few hours in the afternoon to get some work done. I think it's a better way to transition out of here....I might see if Dad will come down after IOP to go to meetings with me and keep me accountable, but maybe not. I don't have an issue with 90 days of meetings as suggested, so I may not bother him. I love you. Please send my love to everyone else and I'll call when I can.
Josh

#3: Hey, Saturday morning here and about to go to a meeting. Had a tough phone call with Avaka yesterday and don't really have anyone else to talk to about it. I did tell my sponsor and some staff about it, but no one that really knows the situation. I told her I wanted to do outpatient the last week here so I'm not thrown out into the world. She said she disagreed and I calmly told her that's fine and I'm willing to stay inpatient but I thought it made sense. Then she said she didn't want me to come home for a <u>year</u>! I'm really just regretting even telling her I needed help. She didn't know there was a problem until I told her and now I'm the worst person ever. I was doing well in here and now I'm so distracted. I just want to leave and get back to my life. There's no sober living or halfway houses here that I can work out of, so there's no real option for much else outside of here. Just AA meetings which I'm fine with. I'm just not willing to lose any more time with the kids, especially if I'm doing what I'm supposed to be doing. So, if she doesn't want to see me for a year, then she can leave and stay at her mom's house. I will watch the kids and go to meetings and she can do whatever she needs to. She's not doing the things that the recovery center is asking her either. She hasn't gone to Al Alon meetings as suggested, or hasn't read the family packet my counselor sent her. ... Anyways, I'm clearly upset and even more upset that I can't focus on my own recovery now. All I can do is think about who's staying and who is going when I get

home. I should have just went to meetings on my own and never told anyone about this. Hope your Mother's Day was good. Josh

I'm stronger spiritually and emotionally than I was 14 years ago when I first discovered the spoon with the burn marks in the bathroom cabinet. It has helped to have almost 12 years of freedom from this dread. First the good stuff. He's communicating with me. He trusts me still to be one who will always love him. Let's take another look at the letters.

Letter #1: Pretty raw and real. Like every addict, they really do want to be a good father and a good husband or a good son or a good brother. They want it. My responsive letter was compassion and encouragement. It was important to tell him that I am not ashamed of him because that is true and he's dealing with shame. Fourteen years ago I was very ashamed of him. I never heard of anyone but skid row junkies doing heroin. Today it's everywhere, a nationwide epidemic. But that's not the reason for my lack of shame. It's because God has taught me to be less judgmental, to live in a grace world and not in a religious world. I hurt for him and his family and our family but it's not shame I'm feeling. It's just genuine sadness for the cost he will pay and anger at the sick people in the world who prey on the weak because their god is money. I shudder at that phrase *I'm officially opiate free today.* That's naive thinking at best. That simply means the medical staff got him through the worst of the detox using a milder form of opiate called *Suboxen* and now have taken him off that. The truth is that heroin will stay in his system for eight to nine months and can suddenly and without warning create a craving he won't be able to resist. This is no longer an irrational decision, it's now a physiological issue. He's not safe.

Letter #2: After two weeks he's more clear-headed. Concerned about lack of contact on Mother's Day. Deals with physical, emotional, and spiritual aspects of healing. Optimistic about the future. Praying. All good. Now the reality. There's still the undercurrent of *I've got this* bleeding through. Willing to go to meetings but not because it's vital to remain clean but because those are the mandatory things he has to check off. *Dad might come down to keep me accountable but maybe not.* Setting up a codependent family member to check on you and watch you is not a good idea. Being accountable to someone is good, but *keeping him* that way still sounds like lack of ownership of his own recovery. The fact that he's trying to get out and thinks he can just slide back into his normal life shows that he very much underestimates the impact this has had on his wife and the serious risk of relapse once he's out on the street facing even more pressure than he was under before.

Letter #3: First response to the impact this has had on his wife and his first sign of loss. This isn't just going to all be fine. Devastated, frightened, but mostly angry. Reaction: blame Avaka. In the fog of a still-heroin-sick mind misrepresenting what happened. He did not tell her voluntarily. He was confronted by a friend who urged him to tell his wife but there were plenty of alarm bells already going off in her mind. Even then he didn't tell her the truth. He confessed only to an addiction to pain killers. A week later she found the needles and the burn spoon in the house while he was responsible for the boys. His lies to me were the same. Pain pills. Some he took by *clean* needles. *Is it heroin, Josh?... No,* he emphatically replied, *Only pain pills.* He got help only because she was being encouraged by me and by Andrea to summon courage through her tears to protect her sons and demand that he get help. Fear is beginning to set in. Loss. Shame. Irresponsible thinking. *I'll take care of the boys and stay in the house.* While sober he was indeed a good dad. Always checking for temps and bumps and taking the kids to the doctor and changing diapers. A good daddy. But when he started using he couldn't see the forest for the trees. He didn't see that he put them in danger by having drugs and needles in the house, leaving oxycodone on the kitchen counter, leaving legal but unsecured handguns in his closet. No, we will all lay down in front of that train. He will not be trusted for a long long time to care for his sons alone. He lost that privilege.

Avaka wrote him a long letter which she shared with me. It was hard to read, hearing how much emotional pain he had caused her and yet also knowing it was all true and that this sweet young man who came out of Haven House ten years ago had morphed back into the angry teen I had lived with. Still, there was love and commitment to him. Clear boundaries and expectations, but love.

I quickly affirmed in a letter what she was telling him. I wrote this letter in about 20 minutes, trying to beat the mail pickup. It flowed out of me. I could not have done this or even believed it 14 years ago. It will hurt him. He counted on me to believe him, to always trust him, to take his side. But to do so may cost him his life and his family. It will have to hurt both of us.

Dear Josh,

Thanks for the Mother's Day message from Bobbie. I appreciated it. Went to church then also to Patty's church where I received a bouquet of flowers and a gift of bath towels with Faith Trust Believe words on them. Nice. Leah & Mike took me to Chevys. In cleaning out storage room this past week I came across a lot of your elementary school writings, several of which were for Mother's Day. So I brought them upstairs and read all the reasons why you loved me at ages 8, 9, and 10. :)

So your time is about up and it's time to talk straight next steps.

I mentioned that I had also watched old videos. It helped me to see you innocent and happy and laughing and kind and caring at those young ages. Before my eyes I could literally see the change in you at about 15. Dropping the F bomb, angry, putting yourself down. The effect of drugs in your life and also in our lives. That was sad. But I remember you having that same kind of childlike sweetness after Haven House. While you had your issues with Chris, being away from old friends and in regular Bible studies restored you to the son I had known. Then the drift happened. Regular drinking. Old anger and defensiveness returning. It's slow and subtle but a slippery slope and one which your family including me should have tried to stop.

I have watched you from a distance and up close. You are good at deception and there have been a lot of lies and I'm very naive, always wanting to believe you. I saw the first signs of trouble on December 23 when you disappeared to go find Bill. I was wondering "Who's Bill and why is this important?" I suspected it then and now we know. So you said to me "it's only been a couple of months, it's not heroin." Once again I wanted to believe you and once again you deceived me. But I know it's heroin talking to me, it's addiction.

I've been worried for some time about how you treat your wife and conduct your life. In FB pics it all looks great. You never want to be accountable to anyone, or said another way, you want to be in total control. You leave without telling anyone, especially your wife, where you are going or when you will return. That has bothered me for my own sake while I was there, never knowing if you could be depended on to show up. It's impossible to have a marriage like that. It isn't normal, respectful, or even remotely kind.

That's not the person Avaka met and fell in love with. I have no idea when or why you began to resent her or fail to appreciate the gift you were given in her. I've even wondered if you actually love her. I can tell you that love is a choice. You can choose to love someone despite their imperfections which we all have or you can choose to focus in on the things you don't like and then pretty soon love is gone because you chose that. I hope and pray you don't make the wrong choice this time. She's too fine a woman to be treated like that. She's much stronger than I was at her age. I stayed in an abusive alcoholic marriage for 25 years, but she won't nor should she. You are at great risk of losing her. And with that you lose your sons, the most precious gift you were ever given.

I say that because I don't sense any real change in your last letter. You don't want to be where you are and you declare you are "100%" and nothing could be further from the truth. Before you ever leave there you are in trouble because you have the mistaken idea that you've got this and you can handle it and just get back to work and go to some AA meetings. Clearly you don't even really want to go to AA meetings, which tells me you aren't desperate to stay clean. You cannot handle it. Heroin is trying to kill you. It will be in your system for eight to nine months and it won't take much to lure you back down that road. The 28 day programs are designed just for the initial stage of detox and getting you to Step 1. That's it. You aren't well, healed, or of sound mind because heroin and whatever thinking led you down that path are still in control.

I think you should be looking at going away for several months to a long-term facility so that you have a fighting chance of saving your life and your family. Or leave the country and go to Slovakia for a few months with your family. Having been through this with you before I know it's the only way. You need to be in a Christian facility where you can really seek out the person of Jesus and get at the root of what causes you to do crazy and risk losing everything. He alone can help you forgive yourself and others, understand your resentments and anger and unkindness toward others. He alone can restore what the devil has stolen from you, your peace of mind, your health, and even your finances. If you love your wife and your sons, you will do whatever it takes to get well so that you can be there for them and actually make their lives better.

I am always, always going to love you. I don't know if you will make the hard choices and if you don't we will lose you, and your wife and children will lose you. And even if you live but make the wrong next step, you will lose everything valuable. The business and the money and houses mean absolutely nothing. Raising your children to be good men of God means everything. Having them love and respect you...everything. Having a wife beside you who truly loves you....everything. Having a close relationship with Jesus, really knowing His love.....everything.

I know this seems harsh. It's not that I don't respect you as a person. I just know that heroin kills and steals and destroys.

Your only hope is restoration through Jesus. He can make you into a man innocent of evil. That kind of change happens when you are desperate for Him. So desperate you read your Bible searching for answers, seek out church services or even listen to great teaching online. I know I'm not the person I was 35 years ago. I was a chronic liar, selfish (though I thought of myself as a martyr), adulterous, untrustworthy, unforgiving, and unkind to many. I hardly recognize that person today. It doesn't seem like it was ever me, but it was. So I know firsthand that God can totally change you. I love my life because my kids and grandkids and friends love me and think highly of me. I didn't get everything I wanted. Never had a marriage to a good man who loved me. But I love my relationships with my kids and grands. I love that I can take mission trips and teach the Word of God. I love that I am at peace almost always, no matter what the circumstances. I love that I am well respected at church and by others who know me. That's a good life. I get the opportunity to make a difference in other people's lives. All my financial needs are met. God restores my health when I get sick. I am a blessed woman.

You can have that and more. You were meant to be one who tells others about Jesus. You were meant to use that great personality that everyone loves to make a difference in the world. I still believe in you. Or said better, I still believe in the God who makes that possible.

God made it simple for us. "I set before you life and death. Choose life."

Praying for you daily.

Easy for me to write this from 850 miles away and being *the backup person* not the main person, appropriately so. Will I be this firm when I talk to him in a few days? God will help me to be as strong and courageous as Avaka is.

Seek First to Understand

Meditate on these truths. No matter what your child's circumstance is today, begin to see yourself doing these things. Then one by one, put them into practice just for today, for right now:

God created me to face and beat any problem I have.

Fear is a spirit - it is cowardly - don't give that to anyone. Speak to it and command it to leave.

Live out of my spirit - listen to the voice of God.

If I live from the inside out there are answers to every problem

Happiness comes from circumstances. Joy is despite circumstances - choose faith.

Anxiety can steal the life I'm living now.

Anxiety isn't based on reality.

Faith & hope are the opposite of anxiety - believing in a good future - it will work out.

Don't worry about anything. Instead, pray.

Focus on what He's already done. Thank Him.

Pray my worries away.

Think right thoughts. I am only responsible for the thoughts I keep - abort the bad thoughts - don't accept them.

Stay in today. Yesterday adds depression and regret. Tomorrow adds anxiety. My mind was designed to live today.

The Promise is peace. Peace guards my mind.

Worry dies in the heights, the Presence of God.

God's Word

For God has not given us a spirit of fear and timidity,
but of power, love and self discipline.
2 Timothy 1:7

Don't worry about anything; instead, pray about everything.
Tell God what you need, and thank Him for all he has done.
Then you will experience God's peace, which exceeds anything we can understand.
His peace will guard your hearts and minds as you live in Christ Jesus.
Philippians 4:6-7

And now, dear brothers and sisters, one final thing. Fix your thoughts
on what is true, and honorable, and right and pure and lovely and admirable.
Think about things that are excellent and worthy of praise.
Philippians 4:8

So don't worry about tomorrow, for tomorrow will bring its own worries.
Today's trouble is enough for today.
Matthew 6:34

Prayer

Thank you, Lord, for giving me your power and love and self-control so that I can choose to reject fear over my child and his choices and instead to believe You said that everything is going to work out. I thank you for providing everything I needed for today. I did not make contact with people I was dreading to talk to. Instead, I had a great time talking about You with my circle of women who know you. Lord, thank you for twelve years of clean living for my son. Thank you for the courage of his wife. Thank you that his children are safe and well cared for. Thank you that he trusts me with what's on his heart both good and bad. I reject the condemnation of the devil that the cause of this is my faulty parenting. I am the righteousness of God in Christ, and all my sins are forgiven and forgotten and I won't remember them either. Father, I am asking as presenting all that Jesus is and did for me, that my child make a wise choice about his next step. Help him to accept responsibility for his choices. Help him find and choose the right place to go when he leaves the recovery center. Help him to see the big picture of being healthy and safe for his children for their whole lives, and to do whatever he needs to do to make that happen. Help him to trust You. Help his wife to seek You. Help me to cast aside every fear and stay in peace. Amen.

THE LION, THE WITCH, AND THE WARDROBE
C. S. Lewis

*"You have a traitor there, Aslan," said the Witch.
Of course everyone present knew that she meant Edmund.
But Edmund had got past thinking about himself after all
he'd been through and after the talk he'd had that morning.
He just went on looking at Aslan. It didn't seem to matter
what the Witch said.*

CHAPTER TWENTY EIGHT

The Presence

There is a meeting today. Avaka, Josh, and his counselor. They will see each other for the first time in a month. She is expecting him to try to manipulate her into a mind change and let him come home. She is prepared for the fight, but unprepared for what actually happened. I so believe in the power of prayer but often don't believe in the power of my own prayers so I gather a team of geographically dispersed warriors to pray for such meetings. Some family members, his sisters and brothers-in-law are covering this meeting. My friend whose own son has relapsed many times is on it. A pastor friend who may not be counted on to show up for a meeting, but can be counted on to pray exactly when asked is covering this meeting. My sister and sister-in-law and my praying-in-the-Spirit buddy from my Wednesday coffee group are covering this meeting. My step-mom is praying, this woman who I am sure has a direct line 24/7. We all do of course, but there is a felt power that surges through me when I hear her pray the Word of God with authority. The power of team. I have prayed for angelic presence in the room where they will meet, for the wisdom and boldness of the Holy Spirit in the counselor, and for calmness and peace over Josh and Avaka. I have also demanded that any spirit of confusion and strife must leave that room.

Of course that spirit doesn't go without a fight. At 11:18, shortly before the meeting is to begin, Josh's dad sends a group text to me, Avaka, the girls and Jim. I know he's hurting but spirits speak through people. The text: *What is going on with my son? No one has bothered to keep me updated in two weeks.* He was sitting at my kitchen table eight days ago spewing the same kind of self-focus and *I know about addiction but no one is asking me.* This is what codependency looks like. I'm left out. It is someone else's responsibility to include me. It's about me. I fight the angry spirit speaking to me right at this moment but do not bite. Avaka is not sucked into the codependency cycle, and she responds kindly that *you have not called me Papa.* She is working full time with a heavy responsibility on her shoulders, but still she kindly gives him time to call her within the hour. He responded with a list of reasons why he cannot make her *call-time windows* and again places the responsibility on her to keep him informed. If we hadn't all been so focused on this critical meeting this might have been laughable. It is a textbook case of someone in recovery who is not dealing with his own issues. I pretended to ignore it, but stewed over it because my first response is to avoid conflict. Andrea texts me frequently asking if I've heard anything…Worry-Warrior. Family members of addicts typically fall back into auto-pilot response in an addiction crisis.

Avaka however, this woman God placed in our family, modeled for *we-who-are-in-hiding-from-codependent-behavior* a textbook response…*We are all busy. If I'm not at work, I'm with kids or taking care of my sick friend, or Josh's business or speaking with the recovery center. My mom calls me every day because she wants to know how I'm doing. Eventually she hits my window. You can call me any* *time after 5:30 every day. I can call you right now but know that you can't just wait on* *others to call you when you wanna know how they are doing, it doesn't work like that.* *Also, to talk to everybody about Josh individually takes a lot of time.* She did what we all must do. Do not accept responsibility for another person. When addiction surfaces in a family even if you've all been through this and think you have been delivered of codependency, it will surface in someone...a parent, a sibling, yourself! It's hard to spot it in yourself. I can talk openly with my girls and both have their ways of letting me see my own unhealthy reaction, just as I can in them. Still I feel a need to read my old notes from <u>My Spiritual Journey</u> and to sign up for the Freedom classes at church this summer. This could be a long journey with Josh and I will need to keep myself emotionally healthy and spiritually healthy and I will need The Great Counselor to do both.

Distractions dealt with, the afternoon passes and the pray-ers have done our job and now wait out the afternoon for any news of the meeting.

The mail comes. A letter from Josh, written on Mother's Day. *Aslan is on the move.* I prayed before I opened it, *Lord, please help me to handle* *anything in this letter.* His last letter was full of anger and victim and *I've got* *this.* Clearly I was anticipating another like it. But God showed up at the recovery center. He knew where Josh was and every thought he had before it became a word on his lips.

> *Hey there. It's Sunday afternoon here and I have found myself with* *lots of free time. I have settled down since my phone conversation with* *Avaka. I'm still not willing to lose any more time with my children, but I've* *accepted that she's at wherever she's at and I can't really do anything about*

it. I don't know what that looks like, but I'll just keep taking care of myself and trying to surrender to God's will. Last time I went through a program, I never really understood that this is a "me disease" and drugs and alcohol are but a symptom. It makes so much sense now and I'm not sure why that never sank in before. I've been trying to run the show and be my own god for as long as I can remember.

I still have to stop and surrender multiple times a day. 'Thy will be done' over and over again. It's a lot easier said than done but I'm in a safe environment to practice. There's so much on the outside that I can't control but again it makes for good practice. It feels good to be praying again. I can feel His Presence more and more.

Later Avaka calls and tells me that the meeting *went good.* Josh was calm. He listened to her. He hugged her. He offered his ideas, which included selling the business and relieving himself of that pressure. He did not close the door on long-term treatment. This report makes perfect and glorious sense in light of his awareness that He needs God and must submit to His will. And that he felt His divine Presence. With the Presence comes peace. I am elated. I want to dance around the room. It's the right step. It's Steps 1, 2, and 3.

Northern winds came down from Canada and brought unseasonable cold on that day. It gave me an excuse to turn on the fireplace in May and sit with my Bible, a hot tea, and this letter. I was pondering the Presence. How like God to just let my son feel Him there with him. I can't recall Josh ever expressing anything like that before. How often do I? I searched for scriptures with the word *presence* and I zeroed in on the account of Moses in Exodus 33:18 *Then show me your glorious presence.* My first reaction was how bold of Moses to ask that of

God. But God wasn't offended. He looked favorably upon Moses and He knew his name. Moses was so filled with the radiance of God that the glow of his face frightened the Israelites and he had to wear a veil to hold their fear at bay. I think that God wants us to ask for His Presence. Perhaps my son did that. Once again God let him know that He knows exactly where he is, and is pleased to be present with him there. Perhaps God knew time in the Presence was necessary to give Moses the courage to go back to Egypt. Perhaps God knew time in the Presence was necessary to give Josh the courage to go out into the world again.

This is what happened to Moses. God announced His Name. *Yahweh. Jehovah. I AM. The self-existent One.* Then while shielding his beloved Moses from more than his flesh could bear, He showed the essence of himself. *All His goodness passed by.* He is good. Totally completely good. Good to us, good for us. Then he described his attributes, how goodness shows up. Mercy, compassion, slow to anger, unfailing love, faithfulness. God gave Josh the fruit of being in his Presence. Psalm 21:6 *You have given him the joy of your presence.*

Just as the Holy Spirit wants to be invited into Josh's bedroom, He wants to be invited to my fireplace seat. The temple veil was broken by the Cross. We can enter into the Presence just by seeking the Lord. I sit by my fireplace on this day and I feel the Presence. In Your Presence there is peace. In Your peace there You are. In Your Presence there is joy. When there is joy there You are. Peace is the absence of strife. It is quiet calm. It is lack of stress. It is rest for my soul.

The Transfiguration is what we have come to call the trip Jesus made to a mountain top with three of his disciples during which he allowed them to see him in his glory. Timothy Keller in his book <u>Jesus</u>

<u>The King</u> says it this way: *Is this Mount Sinai all over again? No, because there's a head-snapping twist. Moses had reflected the glory of God as the moon reflects the light of the sun. But Jesus produces the unsurpassable glory of God; it emanates from Him. Jesus does not point to the glory of God as Elijah, Moses, and every other prophet has done; Jesus is the glory of God in human form.* The author of the book of Hebrews puts it like this: *The Son (Jesus) is the radiance of God's glory and the exact representation of His being (Hebrews 1:3).*

I sit by my fireplace worshipping in my heart and with my words. I repeat God's own words about Himself. He is good. He is mercy. He is compassion. He is unfailing love. He is slow to anger. The peace of God surrounds me. He prepares me for battles yet ahead.

Seek First to Understand

1. What is your child communicating to you right now? What words is he using? Words of hurt or anger or confusion? Words of hope or faith, no matter how slight they may seem?

2. Search the Word of God for what He is saying about that. In the search to understand the state of your child's mind, perhaps God wills to show you how to pray or how to achieve the peaceful calm state you want for yourself today.

God's Word

"I know you by name and I look favorably upon you."
If it is true that you look favorably upon me, let me know your ways so I may
understand you more fully and continue to enjoy your favor.
Exodus 33:12 b - 13

The Lord passed in front of Moses, calling out, "Yahweh! The Lord!
The God of compassion and mercy.
I am slow to anger and filled with unfailing love and faithfulness."
Exodus 34:6

Prayer

My Father, you are good. You have been good to me and to my child. Thank you that You are slow to anger, filled with compassion and mercy, love and faithfulness toward him and toward me. Thank you that You know exactly where he is and You look upon him with favor because of Jesus. He is a child of God and You are slow to anger. You love him. And You love me. You look upon me with favor and You know right where I am. You know where I sit when I'm seeking You. You know when my heart is filled with fear and I am desperate for Your peace. You are merciful to me and You allow Yourself to be found when I seek You. Today Lord, I seek Your Presence. When I am with You all fear is gone. I choose to bless You and worship You today and use Your own words to give You glory. You are good. Amen.

CHAPTER TWENTY NINE

Recovery Stage Two

He has made the decision to stay locally rather than go from Detox/Step One to long-term care. Strangely I feel at peace with this. It wasn't what I wanted. Perhaps I just wasn't ready to face the fear of him being out there again. But he's not a teen any more. Married with children and owner of a business. If he had gone away he would still have had to face all these things when he returned. Met with Wednesday Coffee friends and I clearly heard that God doesn't work on my plan but His. While I was leading a discussion with them about God active in our lives, my mobile phone was actively recording texts between Avaka, Jim, and Andrea. I stayed focused on the task at hand, faith-building coffee talk with my friends. It was clear from the texts that Josh was getting out of rehab within hours. Ready or not, here I come.

Avaka gave us the opportunity to provide input into the contract she has drawn up for Josh to sign. What an honor that is to be trusted. We provided some but she had most of it covered. It's strong, perhaps even demanding, and isn't that exactly what he needs? I recall drawing up a Behavioral Contract based on expectations and rewards when he was maybe 15 or 16. It was weak and I was weak at enforcing. Not this. Dead serious. Fail and lose your family.

He has asked his dad to come down for two weeks to go with him to AA meetings. Good to have a short time limit on it. OK, I feel a little like his dad has been feeling. Left out. He didn't call me. He knew what I would advise (go away) and didn't want to hear it again. Feeling the sting of that this morning I turned to Philippians. I turned Paul's wishes for the Philippians into a specific prayer for Josh and then for Avaka. Philippians 4. There is a promise of joy/rejoicing. How?...Don't worry about anything...Pray. Thank God. Amazing what thankfulness does to your frame of mind.

Father, I thank You that my son is alive today. I thank You for Avaka and her courage. I thank You that the boys are safe. I thank You for family and friends who have compassion and pray for all of us. Thank You that he has a friend who will take him in. Thank You that his dad will go quickly and he is providing something that I cannot provide. Thank You for this very specific agreement.

Wouldn't he be safe if he did all this? Sobriety checks. No secrets. No contact with dangerous friends. A family budget, no more *my money* and *your money*. I have prayed for that. Counseling. Marriage counseling. Church, grow in faith and get involved. God's plan is always better than my plan. Trust God. Trust God. Trust God.

SOBRIETY CONTRACT AGREEMENT

This is a sobriety contract agreement between Josh and Avaka.

This is a simple agreement to establish guidelines of appropriate and acceptable behavior for near future when Josh returns from Recovery. The GOAL of this contract is to stay sober, reunite with the family, provide a safe environment for the children and have a healthy marriage that lasts.

1. I will remain drug and alcohol free. This includes any prescription medication (except for those non-addictive medications approved by PCP for medical conditions), even if prescribed by a doctor. Prescription medicine can only be taken at doctor's approval when necessary. If I use drugs again, I will immediately check in a long term facility and stay there for one year, no questions asked.

2. I will attend a minimum of one daily AA meeting or more if I feel the need for additional support and also counseling at least once a week where I will keep continuing working on dealing with my personal issues.

3. I will have a daily schedule that I will share with my partner and other support (in-laws) and I will follow that schedule. Once I am done with individual counseling and Avaka is willing to join, we will do marital counseling together.

4. If I am not checking in long term facility I will take care of my dog and find him a place to stay other than the house. I will take care of all expenses associated with the dog.

5. I will continue having a sponsor and maintain daily contact with sponsor. If sponsor proves as unavailable/unstable, I will immediately find a new one.

6. Although I said it myself, just as reinforcement written down - If I run into an old *friend*, I will do everything in my power to avoid said *friend*. I will tell them that I am *clean and sober* and do not wish to interact with them. People included are (specific names here). I will unfriend and block all listed contacts and everybody else questionable on any social media/phone. I will contact my sponsor or other support system as soon as possible following any encounters. I will inform Avaka about such encounters too.

7. If I am not checking in a long term facility, I will allow Avaka to handle all money until I can show I can be responsible. If I am given money to take care of necessities and if I do so alone, I will produce the receipt of purchases and correct change back to Avaka. We will develop a working budget together. I will not hide income from Avaka and I will assume fair share of paying common bills.

8. We will co-parent our children and make decisions together, however, the first six months up to one year is my trial period and I have to rely on Avaka's judgment. I will spend time with them only when supervised and not drive them by myself.

9. I will consent to random drug screening as requested by my support system without hesitation or push-back. I will provide body fluid sample for testing anytime upon Avaka's request under close supervision when producing such a fluid sample.

10. We will attend church on Sundays in an effort to renew our faith and develop a friendship with those of like minds. We will take turns on choosing the church and not saying negative things about each other's church in front of kids.

11. I will participate on cleaning the house on Saturday. If for any reason Saturday is not do-able, I will work out with Avaka some other day in that week as a replacement day.

12. We will work on open communication and be honest with each other. We will not hold our honest statements against each other.

13. I will get a new phone number and give my old phone to Avaka. Avaka has a right to check my phones at all times and she will be stated on Sprint as the only authorized Sprint account holder.

14. If I am not moving to long term facility, I am not staying in the house for next year as I am aware I have to prove trustworthy, reliable and safe to be around kids again. If I stay sober for 365 days and the contract is lived up to, I may return home. It may be earlier than that depending on how I am doing – such re-evaluation will happen 180 days after the start of the contract.

If for any reason any of the simple rules are not met, I understand there will be consequences that will be decided upon by my support system to possibly include losing access to my children and possible eviction from the home with no further support from my family. I understand I am responsible for all my actions, and will ask for additional help if I or my family feels it is needed. This contract also has positive consequences for compliance.

I, Josh sign this contract knowing that I cannot always self-evaluate my behaviors, and need the input of others to help keep me in recovery and I will accept the feedback openly.

_____

signature (Josh)

_____

signature (Avaka)

Both Josh and Avaka were required to sign this.

He did not call that night. I felt sad when I went to bed. Next morning he called and I heard his voice and I thanked God throughout the day that he is alive. I wish my emotions were not still so tied to how he's doing. It is what it is and God is changing me daily even when I can't see it or feel it. Once again God has saved his life. He sounded calm and happy, though I know he's coping with a lot of loss. I heard no *victim* or self-pity. We spoke for 30 minutes and then it was time for him to go to an 8 a.m. AA meeting. He had started the day with a devotional. I asked few questions. I have learned that we do better if I don't pummel him with questions. I allow him to share what he wants to share. The only questions I asked had to do with the boys. How was the first reunion? He said Matthew jumped into his arms and said *Daddy, please don't leave.* His voice broke into tears as he told me. My heart ached for both of them. At three and one half years old, Matthew was well aware of his daddy's absence. He loves his daddy so much, but the addict still has to decide to be clean and sober for himself not for anyone else, not even a beloved son. Jeremiah at 17 months doesn't use sentences but wanted to be held the whole time. That's his love language at the moment. Josh stayed for the evening and put them to bed, then left for the room over a garage that will be his home for awhile. This will be their routine every night and it's a good one. Cooking and eating dinner together, play, then bedtime. A Facebook photo of the two boys hugging appeared on his page the next morning *I don't ever want to take for granted what I've been given.*

The first talk. He acknowledged the treatment at the recovery center was good. Many group discussions, presentations by the staff, counseling, and AA meetings. He confessed that until day nine he was fighting it, never intending to stay for a month. Then he changed and began to actually work the program. The doctor told him that 16% of Americans battle addiction because their brains are different. He learned things about his body he hadn't received at 18 and it helped him. He was glad to go to the AA meetings twice a day for 30 days because now it made it easier for him to walk in knowing someone there. We talked briefly about the sobriety contract and trying to encourage him I said, *You know this is just about helping you by providing boundaries.* Yes, he knew, but he also reminded me that the responsibility is his alone to not *pick up*. I guess that's user jargon. I hate all things about that but refusing to think about it or hear it is codependent behavior. A national TV station is airing segments every night this week about a young man and his brother both addicted to heroin and using any drug they can get their hands on. I didn't want to watch it but I did. Deal with it, Lee. This was my son's daily life just four weeks ago. Thinking about drugs from the moment he woke up and how to get them. I can't really understand it. This is why he needed his father to come down. He would understand the craving through his struggle.

Amazing how calm and joyous I felt all day. I will not feel bad for these emotions that are mine. Yes, it's much easier to feel peaceful when hope is accompanied by a day without fear. But the time I've spent in quiet trusting prayer this month has built a foundation of joy. God can be trusted no matter the circumstances. There will be good days and bad. Seedtime and harvest. There is a good future because the Lord is in it. Today I celebrate. He is alive and well today. This is my daily bread.

Seek to Understand

1. Suddenly we are bombarded by stories about heroin use in America, in our state, in our neighborhood. Our middle class neighbors are holding anti-heroin marches. Our local police departments are overwhelmed, dedicating resources to an epidemic, and their squad cars are now carrying life-saving Naloxone to reverse effects of an overdose. Private recovery centers are making a fortune. Non-profit ones are often full/no bed available. In the last 12 years heroin has gone from urban junkie to suburban your son and mine and the kid or the

businessman next door and we are no longer stunned to hear it. Parents are not bad people but ordinary. Every family affected and infected by drug addiction, whether to heroin or meth or crack or opioids, will wrestle with Recovery Step Two. They are out of the safe place and now they are ours to deal with. How do we deal? I certainly never had a written contract ten or twelve years ago. There was hope and a lot of fear, but there was no signed agreement. While I praise God for Avaka and her strength, I wonder if it was me alone, could I have done this?

2. Whether you are in the driver's seat or the back seat, what would you write in the sobriety contract for your child? What's the goal of sober living? What's really important to God? Are there benchmarks for success? Are they possible to meet on your timetable? Do they cover spiritual, emotional, and physical improvement?

3. Begin to write them down for the day when you will need them. Pray over them as the Holy Spirit brings new understanding to your mind. Ask God to give you courage just to do your part. Ask him for more of His grace to see His will and His desires for your child.

God's Word

Our Father in Heaven, may your name be kept holy
May your Kingdom come soon
May your will be done on earth as it is in Heaven.
Give us today the food we need
and forgive us our sins
as we have forgiven those who trespass against us.
And don't let us yield to temptation
but rescue us from the evil one.
Matthew 6:9-13

My Prayer

My Father, you are sovereign. You are seated on Your throne and You see and understand all things. I honor You today. I want what You want. May Your peace and love and joy come down from Heaven into each of our lives today. Thank You that my child wants Your will and Your way for his life. I am grateful that You give me exactly what I need for today. Today my child is alive and safe. Today he has a family who loves him. Today I have children and grandchildren who love me. All my children are fed and sheltered and drawing closer to you. Today I have a cozy home and a Bible to which I retreat and am at rest. Lord, I am forgiven of my fears and angry tongue just as I forgive my ex-husband for his angry outbursts and hurt feelings. He responded to his son's needs quickly and I am grateful. I ask that my child be kept safe from the temptations of the world today. Thank you that he is going to AA meetings every day and making himself accountable. Thank you that once again You rescue him and also me from the evil one who has tried to stop us from pursuing You and being available for Your plans. You are good. Amen.

My friend, There will be times of respite from chaos and fear. You will not know when or if another season of struggle may come. Remember to thank God for all that is good and positive in your family's life. Recognize the goodness of God always.

CHAPTER THIRTY

The Dance

*J*ust as God put this into your hands because you needed it, so He will bring who or what you need when you need it to move you along on this journey to healing. As I was just learning about Josh's relapse and was also struggling with anemia and neuropathy (no energy, constant pain) a friend sent me a book called Jesus The King written by Timothy Keller. In my weakness I had difficulty focusing on reading and I set it aside. Then one day I just picked it up and could hardly put it down. My early thoughts were *Oh, Josh should read this!* I recognized my son's behavior but I also saw my own. Seek first to understand *me*. The author gets to the core of relationship with Jesus and how it's been showing up in my son's life and my own. To walk through the stages of relapse and recovery will require me to get back to the core of what I believe about my own relationship with Jesus The King.

Jesus came from Nazareth in Galilee and was baptized by John in the Jordan.
As Jesus was coming up out of the water, he saw heaven being torn open
and the Spirit descending on him like a dove. And a voice came from heaven:
"You are my Son, whom I love; with you I am well pleased."
Mark 1:9-11.

Timothy Keller quotes theologian Cornelius Plantinga: *"Each divine person harbors the others at the center of his being. In constant movement of overture and acceptance, each person envelops and encircles the others...God's interior life therefore overflows with regard for others."* He adds when it's a person you find beautiful in that way, you want to serve them unconditionally. When you say, *"I'll serve as long as I'm getting benefits from it"* then that's not actually serving people. It's serving yourself through them. That's not circling them, orbiting around them; it's using them, getting them to orbit around you. If we can't say no but only yes, others say we are so selfless. But for those of us who don't have boundaries and let people walk all over us and use us and can't say no...that is not *regard for others.* We are doing it out of need, out of fear and cowardice. A self-centered person wants to be the center around which everything else orbits. Self-centeredness makes everything else a means to an end. And that end is whatever I want and whatever I like, my interests over theirs.

Self-giving love. Make yourself totally vulnerable and you orbit around other people. I see my son's struggle. If he let his wife expect something normal from him like announcing where he's going and when he'll return, then he gives up control. If he gives up control then he is vulnerable to being hurt. Satan tells him that's crazy, you don't have to do that. You can be the one in control all the time. The father of lies and the spirit of fear. Why this fear? Certainly he was hurt as a child. He says the divorce of his parents didn't bother him but it was actually devastating. He was the object of a power struggle in court. Who would raise him? What money would go to whom? Who is the *bad guy* in this divorce? Who will win? No one wins of course, and the children suffer. It's a by-product of addiction. Broken families, broken hearts. Insecurities. Not feeling smart. Not able to articulate opinions and then being frustrated and angry. And I want to shout at him *God is crazy about you. He put wonderful things in you. Run to Him.* But he has to enter the dance himself. I cannot change the past and must fix my eyes on the things God has yet to accomplish through me on earth. I can pray that God will help him work through the 12 steps and give him a good counselor that can help him dig out the painful spots, forgive, recognize how they impacted his marriage and other relationships, and leave them with Jesus in a healed spot. But I cannot do it for him or even help him with that. Trust God and move on, Leejae.

There are stages of recovery for me just like there are for those kids we love. At first I just wanted him in a safe place and my cry was *Lord, save his life!* He did and I am overwhelmed with thankfulness. While he was in that cocoon of the recovery center I was thinking about the motivations of my own heart, the what and why of this mother/son relationship. Everyone in the extended family knew about his battle with drug addiction though not everyone knew it was heroin twelve years ago. He is one of those people everyone likes and when I ran into family I seldom saw there was always that low-voice, look-into-my-eyes, fearful question *How is Josh?* And I gladly told them he was doing great then I described *great*. Married, two sons, two houses, owns his own business, goes to church....great! And they were relieved and we moved on. Why did I always feel a need to define it and why use those examples? Because that's the way we define *great* in our American culture. The emphasis is on outward signs of prosperity and success. That's how I see my own self-centeredness. I need him to be well so I can be well. I need to brag about him because he reflects me. My life is worry-free. I can be deeply spiritual, concentrating on other God projects. Really loving him means continually seeing the good in him when it isn't lining up with *success*. It also means saying *no* when that's what he actually needs. And how will I answer that question now when asked? *How is Josh?* They will ask slowly as if they will get an answer they don't want or details they don't want to know. *He's doing great!* And that's all they need to know. What God started in him He will continue. Josh will bring glory to God because the Lord is able to do that. He may show it in his life so that *others* will know, or he may reveal it to the Lord alone. What could be better? To the glory of God.

Now I redefine *great* for both of us as being whole. Spiritually whole. Checking in with God continuously. Doing things His way. Being at peace. Finding contentment in knowing how much He loves us. Entering the dance with Him. Out of the fountain of love really loving others not so *we* can get our needs met but so *they* can because we are inviting them into the dance of love. Emotionally whole. No longer manipulating others for our own purposes. Walking in integrity and speaking only truth. Hiding nothing because there's nothing to hide. Physically well. I don't know what damage has been done to his liver. I do know that Jesus provided for our salvation and our healing on the cross. All things are possible and I will trust God for the healing of our bodies. Twelve years ago the doctors said there was no cure for Hepatitis C that he had contracted by sharing needles with a friend who died of overdose. But the right combination of meds were found. For six months he got weekly shots and took meds every day. It was costly and he paid for it himself. He took me out to breakfast during a trip to Florida and quietly shared it with me. He was free of it. I was stunned that he had done this and I never knew. Why do I ever doubt God? Didn't I pray for this? Lord, I believe! Help my unbelief!

The stuff we own means nothing. I know this but how quickly I let it creep in. If he lived in a tiny house with his family and relieved the pressure of debt wouldn't I be happy? If they sold it all and became transient missionaries, wouldn't I be happy? Whatever the dance looks like for him, I would celebrate and probably brag about it and the Holy Spirit would check me on that, too. For today, he sleeps in a room over a garage and takes a shower in an outside wooden building where he can see the sky and trees. The future of the two houses and businesses and relationships is unknown to me. And that's OK. Because I'm in the dance with Jesus and at peace. Years ago I had visions of me dancing before the Throne of God. Jesus proudly escorted me in and then watched as I danced like a prima ballerina before our Father. I was young and beautiful and leaping and exquisite in every graceful move. At 70 and battling polyneuropathy, that is not my current physical condition. This I know: I am celebrated by God. He loves me. *Celebrating God on earth with my whole heart is the dance.* The vision will come to pass at the appointed time.

Seek First to Understand

1. What or who is God putting before you to stretch you, to help you think clearly? Are you able to separate your own walk with God from your child's? If not, stop where you are and pray, giving him over to God and asking God to show you how He's thinking about you. Write down how you would define success for your child's life on earth. Find a scripture that speaks to that definition. Pray it over your child. Set it aside.

2. Who has God brought into your life to talk this out with utter confidentiality? Are there books, websites, sermons, that are causing you to think differently about your situation? Notice them. Thank God for them.

3. Have you entered the dance? Are you experiencing rushes of love from God? Do you find yourself more able to love the unlovable ones in your life? Define the finish line for your own life. Find a scripture that speaks to that goal. Pray it over yourself.

God's Word

I press on to possess that perfection for which Christ Jesus first possessed me.
No, dear brothers and sisters, I have not achieved it, but I focus on this one thing:
forgetting the past and looking forward to what lies ahead.
I press on to reach the end of the race and receive the heavenly prize
for which God, through Christ, is calling us.
Philippians 3:12-14

Teach us to realize the brevity of life, so that we may grow in wisdom.
Psalm 90:12

David danced before the Lord with all his might.
2 Samuel 6:14a

Prayer

Father, I choose to focus my mind on Jesus and the glory I will enjoy with Him when my assignment on earth is complete. I want to keep becoming more like Him. I want to notice and celebrate the people you have assigned to me to disciple. I want to use all the gifts you have given me and leave none of them to dust. Thank you for dealing with my past and all the cares that want to drag me backward or stop me in my tracks. I embrace this day and every person I encounter. Let me show them Jesus. I lift up my eyes to the one thing that matters. I choose to enter the dance with You. Amen.

THE LION, THE WITCH, AND THE WARDROBE
C. S. Lewis

Edmund was on the other side of Aslan, looking all the time at Aslan's face. He felt a choking feeling and wondered if he ought to say something; but a moment later he felt that he was not expected to do anything except to wait, and do what he was told.

CHAPTER THIRTY ONE

The Hundred

Who are you to judge another master's servant?
It's to his own master he stands or falls,
and he will stand because the Lord is able to make him stand.
Romans 14:4

A month after his re-entry into his daily life in Santa Rosa Beach I was on the ground in Florida. I told myself going down that I had no expectations of what would happen. I was there to celebrate his 32nd birthday and his life and my love for him. That part was true, but the reality was that I expected him to be happy and the two of us to have deep, meaningful, and spiritual talks. Maybe he would even make amends for the lies, the money, the disappointment. Within hours around him I felt those old codependent feelings rushing back. He was quiet, even crabby. We had dinner together, fireworks with the kids, and then he went to his small garage apartment to sleep. The next night about the same. After an evening AA meeting he came for a late dinner and to put the kids to bed and left soon after. Now my radar is swirling into overdrive. Negative thoughts. Fearful thoughts. He's sullen when he's using. What if he is already using? Am I blind to it again? I tried to pray but I was yielding to my fears. A late night talk with Avaka made me even more anxious and I'm sure I fueled her fears.

The next night Avaka played out her fears. When he came in she immediately handed him a pee cup. These things were easier to do when I was present. Part of their signed agreement of sobriety included her testing his urine for drugs anytime she asked. He gave it to her without hesitation. It was negative. Then she took his phone and checked all his text messages and emails, also part of the agreement. Nothing to find. There was so much tension in the air I could hardly stand it. I also couldn't just run to the bedroom and hide out. He was embarrassed. The honeymoon of not being kicked out of his family was over and now there was just plain hard work of reestablishing trust. He said later that he's doing everything he agreed to do but it's not enough for her, and that she treats him a lot better when I'm there. She clearly doubts his love for her and is terribly afraid that her mother will be proven right. It's a dark place to be. She wonders out loud if there is some hot chick at the AA meetings who will understand him better. I held her hands and prayed that night. Physically exhausted, I fell into bed leaving her filling out the marriage questionnaire for their counseling appointment the following day.

Third day. I finally asked him when he stopped by at lunch if he was okay. I expressed my concern about his somber and irritable attitude and expressions of *overwhelmed* and *stress*. He did not react well. He said I was adding to his stress because he felt like I came there to watch him. I denied it because I didn't think it was true. But it was true that I came there with expectations of la-la land. We would laugh and share. That was not happening. Codependency involves trying to control another person and then internalizing it when you can't. And you always can't. True to form I had also already expressed my concerns to his two sisters. Why am I remaking the same mistakes? Twelve years ago God showed me that kings reveal things but God conceals them. That's about me not trusting God and instead venting my emotions with family members. I know better and still I'm accelerating down the same bumpy hill.

By six the next morning I was up with my Bible and coffee on the screened in porch. Praying for God's help to say and do right things and be quiet when I need to be. Looking at my underlined scriptures. Beginning to get back to *normal* and getting those hormones flowing back into their respective reservoirs. I was enjoying my time with the boys. We did finger paint. Playtime on the floor. Books. Shopping for their daddy's birthday gifts at the Dollar General. Trips to the water park. Lunch with their daddy at his print shop.

They were both in a better place after their counseling appointment. Getting the junk out that we have buried is still a healing balm even when there aren't easy steps to changing ourselves or gaining understanding from your partner in life. After the boys were in bed he stayed for awhile and began to talk about his work pressures. It was good news really. He had landed two major new customers. But he would need a larger, expensive new press with more automation and a bigger space. He had already priced them and negotiated a larger space in the same building. He would need to quit his part time work at the coffee shop which is impossible right now because the home of the coffee shop owner is where he's sleeping! I'm relieved that he's trying to talk to me. Avaka never rejoined us after putting the baby to sleep so he went to his sleeping quarters.

A breakthrough for me came on Saturday morning when I went to my first AA meeting with him. I was surprised to walk into a room of about a hundred men and women. Some had driven a couple of hours to be there. I met Adam, the intake director from the recovery center. He was truly pleased with how Josh was doing. After the opening readings the remainder of the meeting was spent with the alcoholics or drug addicts taking a few minutes to talk about how working the steps is helping them. Most told a brief history of their addiction history. Many told about how they dealt with a problem recently and reacted differently than they would have when using either alcohol or drugs. They were funny but also greatly encouraging. Each person was following a pattern: the chaos of my life on drugs or alcohol, what happened to put me on a different path, and how my life is better now. All were talking about God as their helper. Their testimony. Their story.

Immediately I recalled how I felt when I first visited the Boonville Missouri Recovery Center where he first went for treatment. The patients were relaxed with each other, though much less so with uncomfortable parents and spouses arriving. Josh felt safe here in this room, they all did. No one in this room was judging them. No one was staring at them, checking them out. All were encouraging one another. I remember one of the men saying that being here was like walking into *normal*. With no warning Josh's friend Peter, who was at the Recovery Center with him, called on my son to speak. He didn't hesitate even with me there. *I'm Josh and I'm an alcoholic. What I have learned this time that I should have understood before but didn't is that my problem is not alcohol or drugs. My problem is that I'm not a happy person. But working the steps is helping.*

I hated to hear that he is not a happy person. But truly, are any of us happy people without embracing the love of God for us and realizing that we are not a mistake. We were made by our Creator exactly as we are. Each of us seeking the Lord and understanding of Truth will doubt that at times when our world is rocked but He never quits on us and He won't quit on my son or on me. Everyone in that room, including me, has had trouble believing that we are truly forgiven because Satan wants us to focus on our past and our shame. Freedom comes by regularly being reminded of our need for God and His willingness and ability to lift those burdens. In that room I felt freedom and grace. A hundred men and women who have felt the Presence of Grace and extended it to others. I became acutely aware of that lesson God taught me many years ago. I am this man's mother but I am not his judge. He answers only to his Creator. My judgment hurts him and makes him want to distance himself from me. None of us enjoys being with someone who is looking down on us. I wish I could just learn this once and have it in me forever but it rarely works this way. We need reminding.

The meeting closed with all of us holding hands in a big circle saying the Lord's Prayer. It is that universal prayer for Christians of all denominations. I was surprised that all embraced God and it was okay to say it. After that meeting we went to breakfast with Peter and his wife and two young sons, another couple and an older gentleman. It was an atmosphere of kindness and concern for one another. It was normal. The world without God at the center is not normal. The hundred showed me the way we are supposed to accept one another. God's Word tells us to speak to one another in truth and love. They didn't need to pretend with each other. Truth. No matter what ugly glimpse they give their fellow travelers into their past lives, they are still loved. This makes Jesus happy.

The two of us sat alone at a restaurant on the morning of his birthday. There was only peace and joy between us as we celebrated his life. *What have you learned about yourself that you didn't know before?* I asked. Quietly but without hesitation he answered, *I wanted to be my own God. I'm not Him. Now I start every day asking for His will to be done in my life. It's not easy because I still want my way.* That is the pathway to peace and God speaks in that quiet voice to my own heart.

Seek First to Understand

1. Before we can overflow with love no matter the circumstances we have to first be healed in our own soul. It may be like peeling back an onion. You thought you had but then another layer needs to go. That's okay.

2. We all have a story. Does your story include a critical parent or spouse? Can you still easily recall the stinging words or actions?

3. What steps might you need to take to forgive them in your heart and let that pain go? Possible resources to help you in that process are listed at the end of this book.

4. Recall the moment when you first understood what Jesus had done for you on the cross and received him. Close your eyes and relive it.

5. Walk back in time when your son or daughter was four. Feel the joy of a special time you had together. Rest your mind on the peacefulness of looking at that sleeping little face. Picture Jesus looking down at his sleeping face even now.

God's Word

*Instead, we will speak the truth in love, growing in every way more and more
like Christ, who is the head of his body, the church.*
Ephesians 4:15

*It has come at last--salvation and power and the kingdom of our God
and the authority of his Christ.*
*For the accuser of our brothers and sisters has been thrown down to earth—
the one who accuses them before our God day and night.*
*And they have defeated him by the blood of the Lamb
and the word of their testimonies.*
Revelation 12: 10-11a

Prayer

Father, thank you for the gift of Jesus and forgiving me of my sins. Thank you for loving me and my child. I extend grace to him as Your child just as both You and he have extended it to me. Lord, heal me in my spirit, soul, and body. Teach me to walk in freedom and to speak the truth in love to my child and all those you bring into my path. In Christ, Amen.

THE LION, THE WITCH, AND THE WARDROBE
C.S. Lewis

"We have a long journey to go. You must ride on me." And he crouched down and the children climbed onto his warm, golden back, and Susan sat first, holding on tightly to his mane and Lucy sat behind holding on tightly to Susan. And with a great heave he rose underneath them and then shot off, faster than any horse could go, down hill and into the thick of the forest.

CHAPTER THIRTY TWO

Two Jalapenos Not One!

More than a month later, I am back to life with my Wednesday women, church youth, family and friends. My health is slowly improving. I'm taking on a new voluntary assignment for international missions administration. Josh and I talk on the phone or Facetime two or three times a week. He is still sleeping in the over-garage bedroom and at home with family in the evenings. Avaka now trusts him to be alone with the boys and he watches them frequently while she's at work or running errands. They are together on weekend days, cleaning house, cooking, or going on family outings.

They go to marriage counseling every couple of weeks. I asked how that was going without pressing for details. He shared a few ups and downs. At their most recent session she vented to the counselor about her example of his selfishness and lack of concern for her. *He was making homemade salsa and he put two jalapenos in the salsa knowing that I don't like it that hot and would have only wanted one!* Isn't that just as silly as the things we argue about in our own relationships? In truth most of our fights are about trivial things which disguise our real inner issues. The counselor wisely but without judgment asked her what would have happened if she had asked or even told Josh that she would like him to make the salsa with only one jalapeno rather than assume he knew that. Letting our wants be known to another person, especially to a spouse or other significant person, is one of the building blocks of healthy relationships. Both of them have to first know themselves and trust the other person for this to happen.

This applies to the mother-son relationship as well. You may be accustomed to walking on eggshells around him. You are afraid to ask him hard questions because he may get angry. Or afraid that if you tell him what you need from him that it will feel like a controlling demand and that won't go well either. This is all harder work when trust has been broken. But learn it you must. Ask what you really need to know. Tell him what helps you relax and not worry, e.g., returning phone calls. And listen carefully when he tells you what he needs...*stop staring at me like you are checking me out every time I see you.* Remember that recovery is hard work for everyone involved. New communication skills need to be learned. It feels good.

God forgives us our sins but there are still consequences for our choices and He won't often remove those because we won't learn otherwise.

I hear a maturity in him that I haven't heard before. I asked how much longer it would be until he gets to move home. He responded that it will be at least six months because that's what he committed to in their contract. He knows that if he pressed her he would be successful and could shortcut that even now. Remarkably he added, *She needs to win. If I do that to her she will feel like she has lost.* He will continue to take his showers in a wooden outdoor shower shed and hope he's home before it gets cold. It is a level of unselfishness and understanding I don't recall in him. Every step matters.

He's looking forward to another visit from his dad. He enjoys his company. They have plans to go to a local football game and choose their Fantasy Football teams. It is my natural tendency as a divorced parent even of grown children to want to protect them from every hurt. I imagined that the angry person on the other end of the phone with me would behave the same way with his son and I wanted to protect my man-child from that hurt. I was wrong. James was right when he said that he understood what Josh was going through more than any of us. I may understand that mentally but I can never understand it emotionally, that bond of brotherhood between two men in recovery, much less how healing takes place when they are watching a football game together with few words exchanged. The U.S. Department of Health and Human Services states, "Fatherless children are at a dramatically greater risk of drug and alcohol abuse." If you are a single mom, recognize the important role of the biological father in your child's recovery. That's a very general statement and many circumstances may dictate whether the father is able and willing to assume his role. Remember the only person you can control is yourself. So as much as it depends on you, get yourself out of the way and let them be in each other's lives if they choose to be. I thank God that His ways are not my ways. He knows best. Yet one more lesson for me.

There are strained relationships with in-laws. Broken or wounded relationships extend well beyond the marriage. Trust must be earned and it's a slow process. I encouraged him to just continue to show respect and love. His AA sponsor and the group meetings are vital for him to have a sounding board. Others have walked across these hot stones. They will not give him pity but remind him that these are consequences of his choices. Make the right choice today, for this day only.

A friend watched the boys so he and Avaka could take a kayak trip on a river with friends. They drank coconut water instead of beer. He described it as a great time. He had never made this river trip sober and it was more fun sober. He posted a picture of the two of them in a sweet kiss on the riverbank. I treasure this. God is the restorer of our souls and our brokenness.

His commitment was to attend 90 AA meetings in 90 days. That period is now over. I asked him how often he will be going to meetings now. He said *Every day. I will not change anything. I need them.*

I am attending a 12-week small group called Freedom. Last week the planned discussion outlined the areas we will explore in depth. Selfishness. Bitterness. Rejection. Evil Thoughts. When I heard the word *rejection* I wanted to bolt for the door and not return. That tells me that this onion peeling is needed. God will continue to perfect those things in me that he started working on decades ago. It may hurt but He wants me totally free of any burden that keeps me from doing the very good and important work he planned for me.

We have a life to live, you and I. We were never meant to live our lives tethered to our children. They have their own lives to walk out and He will guide them safely through if they will turn back to the One you taught them about. God has given you and me gifts. They will put us in position to draw others nearer to Him. Having walked across the hot stones of addiction with a child, we are uniquely equipped to extend grace and mercy to others whose lives are not Facebook perfect. They are embarrassed and ashamed. They are fearful. We will hold their hands and share our stories. God is good. He is faithful. He is all powerful. There is hope for the end of their story as there is for yours.

Jesus began a good work in you and and your child. He will continue to complete it until the day He returns for you both.

Aslan is on the Move.

THE LION, THE WITCH, AND THE WARDROBE
C. S. Lewis

He had become his real old self again and could look you in the face.
And there on the field of battle Aslan made him a knight.

APPENDIX A

A Spiritual Journey

THE TWELVE STEPS AND RELATED SCRIPTURE

STEP ONE

We admitted we were powerless over the effects of our separation from God--that our lives had become unmanageable.

I know nothing good lives in me, that is, in my sinful nature.
For I have the desire to do what is good, but I cannot carry it out.
Romans 7:18

STEP TWO

Came to believe that a power greater than ourselves could restore us to sanity.

For it is God who works in you to will and to act according to his good purpose
Philippians 2:13

STEP THREE

Made a decision to turn our will and our lives over to the care of God as we understood Him.

Therefore, I urge you brothers, in view of God's mercy,
to offer your bodies a living sacrifice, holy and pleasing to God —
which is your spiritual worship.
Romans 12:1

STEP FOUR

Made a searching and fearless moral inventory of ourselves.

Let us examine our ways and test them, and let us return to the Lord.
Lamentations 3:40

STEP FIVE

Admitted to God, to ourselves, and to another human being the exact nature of our wrongs.

Therefore, confess your sins to each other and pray for each other
so that you may be healed.
James 3:16a

STEP SIX

Were entirely ready to have God remove all these defects of character.

Humble yourselves before the Lord, and he will lift you up
James 4:10

STEP SEVEN

Humbly asked Him to forgive our shortcomings.

If we confess our sins, he is faithful and just and will forgive us our sins
and purify us from all unrighteousness.
I James 1:9

STEP EIGHT

Made a list of all persons we had harmed and became willing to make amends to them all.

Do to others as you would have them do to you.
Luke 6:31

STEP NINE

Made direct amends to such people wherever possible, except when to do so would injure them or others.

Therefore, if you are offering your gift at the altar and there remember that your brother
has something against you, leave your gift there in front of the altar.
First go and be reconciled to your brother; then come and offer your gift.
Matthew 5:23-24

STEP TEN

Continued to take personal inventory and, when we were wrong, promptly admitted it.

So, if you think you are standing firm, be careful that you don't fall.
1 Corinthians 10:12

STEP ELEVEN

Sought through prayer and meditation to improve our conscious contact with God as we understood Him, praying only for knowledge of His will for us and the power to carry that out.

Let the word of Christ dwell in you richly.
Colossians 3:16a

STEP TWELVE

Having had a spiritual awakening as the result of these steps, we tried to carry this message to others, and to practice these principles in all our affairs.

Brothers, if someone is caught in a sin, you who are spiritual should restore him gently.
But watch yourself, or you also may be tempted.
Galatians 6:1

Appendix B

Understanding Addiction

How Addiction Hijacks the Brain

Addiction involves craving for something intensely, loss of control over its use, and continuing involvement with it despite adverse consequences. Addiction changes the brain, first by subverting the way it registers pleasure and then by corrupting other normal drives such as learning and motivation. Although breaking an addiction is tough, it can be done.

What causes addiction?

The word "addiction" is derived from a Latin term for "enslaved by" or "bound to." Anyone who has struggled to overcome an addiction—or has tried to help someone else to do so—understands why.

Addiction exerts a long and powerful influence on the brain that manifests in three distinct ways: craving for the object of addiction, loss of control over its use, and continuing involvement with it despite adverse consequences.

For many years, experts believed that only alcohol and powerful drugs could cause addiction. Neuroimaging technologies and more recent research, however, have shown that certain pleasurable activities, such as gambling, shopping, and sex, can also co-opt the brain.

Although a standard U.S. diagnostic manual (the *Diagnostic and Statistical Manual of Mental Disorders, Fourth Edition* or DSM-IV) describes multiple addictions, each tied to a specific substance or activity, consensus is emerging that these may represent multiple expressions of a common underlying brain process.

New insights into a common problem

Nobody starts out intending to develop an addiction, but many people get caught in its snare. Consider the latest government statistics:

- Nearly 23 million Americans—almost one in 10—are addicted to alcohol or other drugs.
- More than two-thirds of people with addiction abuse alcohol.
- The top three drugs causing addiction are marijuana, opioid (narcotic) pain relievers, and cocaine.

In the 1930s, when researchers first began to investigate what caused addictive behavior, they believed that people who developed addictions were somehow morally flawed or lacking in willpower. Overcoming addiction, they thought, involved punishing miscreants or, alternately, encouraging them to muster the will to break a habit.

The scientific consensus has changed since then. Today we recognize addiction as a chronic disease that changes both brain structure and function. Just as cardiovascular disease damages the heart and diabetes impairs the pancreas, addiction hijacks the brain. This happens as the brain goes through a series of changes, beginning with recognition of pleasure and ending with a drive toward compulsive behavior.

Pleasure principle

The brain registers all pleasures in the same way, whether they originate with a psychoactive drug, a monetary reward, a sexual encounter, or a satisfying meal. In the brain, pleasure has a distinct signature: the release of the neurotransmitter dopamine in the nucleus accumbens, a cluster of nerve cells lying underneath the cerebral cortex (see illustration). Dopamine release in the nucleus accumbens is so consistently tied with pleasure that neuroscientists refer to the region as the brain's pleasure center.

All drugs of abuse, from nicotine to heroin, cause a particularly powerful surge of dopamine in the nucleus accumbens. The likelihood that the use of a drug or participation in a rewarding activity will lead to addiction is directly linked to the speed with which it promotes dopamine release, the intensity of that release, and the reliability of that release.

Even taking the same drug through different methods of administration can influence how likely it is to lead to addiction. Smoking a drug or injecting it intravenously, as opposed to swallowing it as a pill, for example, generally produces a faster, stronger dopamine signal and is more likely to lead to drug misuse.

Brain's Reward Center

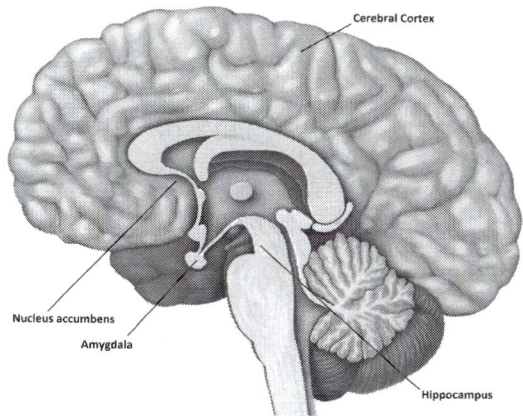

Addictive drugs provide a shortcut to the brain's reward system by flooding the nucleus accumbens with dopamine. The hippocampus lays down memories of this rapid sense of satisfaction, and the amygdala creates a conditioned response to certain stimuli.

Learning process

Scientists once believed that the experience of pleasure alone was enough to prompt people to continue seeking an addictive substance or activity. But more recent research suggests that the situation is more complicated. Dopamine not only contributes to the experience of pleasure, but also plays a role in learning and memory—two key elements in the transition from liking something to becoming addicted to it.

According to the current theory about addiction, dopamine interacts with another neurotransmitter, glutamate, to take over the brain's system of reward-related learning. This system has an important role in sustaining life because it links activities needed for human survival (such as eating and sex) with pleasure and reward.

The reward circuit in the brain includes areas involved with motivation and memory as well as with pleasure. Addictive substances and behaviors stimulate the same circuit—and then overload it.

Repeated exposure to an addictive substance or behavior causes nerve cells in the nucleus accumbens and the prefrontal cortex (the area of the brain involved in planning and executing tasks) to communicate in a way that couples liking something with wanting it, in turn driving us to go after it. That is, this process motivates us to take action to seek out the source of pleasure.

Do you have addiction?

Determining whether you have addiction isn't completely straightforward. And admitting it isn't easy, largely because of the stigma and shame associated with addiction. But acknowledging the problem is the first step toward recovery.

A *yes* answer to any of the following three questions suggests you might have a problem with addiction and should—at the very least—consult a health care provider for further evaluation and guidance.

- Do you use more of the substance or engage in the behavior more often than in the past?
- Do you have withdrawal symptoms when you don't have the substance or engage in the behavior?
- Have you ever lied to anyone about your use of the substance or extent of your behavior?

Development of tolerance

Over time, the brain adapts in a way that actually makes the sought-after substance or activity less pleasurable.

In nature, rewards usually come only with time and effort. Addictive drugs and behaviors provide a shortcut, flooding the brain with dopamine and other neurotransmitters. Our brains do not have an easy way to withstand the onslaught.

Addictive drugs, for example, can release two to 10 times the amount of dopamine that natural rewards do, and they do it more quickly and more reliably. In a person who becomes addicted, brain receptors become overwhelmed. The brain responds by producing less dopamine or eliminating dopamine receptors—an adaptation similar to turning the volume down on a loudspeaker when noise becomes too loud.

As a result of these adaptations, dopamine has less impact on the brain's reward center. People who develop an addiction typically find that, in time, the desired substance no longer gives them as much pleasure. They have to take more of it to obtain the same dopamine "high" because their brains have adapted—an effect known as tolerance.

Compulsion takes over

At this point, compulsion takes over. The pleasure associated with an addictive drug or behavior subsides—and yet the memory of the desired effect and the need to recreate it (the wanting) persists. It's as though the normal machinery of motivation is no longer functioning.

The learning process mentioned earlier also comes into play. The hippocampus and the amygdala store information about environmental cues associated with the desired substance, so that it can be located again. These memories help create a conditioned response—intense craving—whenever the person encounters those environmental cues.

Cravings contribute not only to addiction but to relapse after a hard-won sobriety. A person addicted to heroin may be in danger of relapse when he sees a hypodermic needle, for example, while another person might start to drink again after seeing a bottle of whiskey. Conditioned learning helps explain why people who develop an addiction risk relapse even after years of abstinence.

Recovery is possible

It is not enough to "just say no"—as the 1980s slogan suggested. Instead, you can protect (and heal) yourself from addiction by saying "yes" to other things. Cultivate diverse interests that provide meaning to your life. Understand that your problems usually are transient, and perhaps most importantly, acknowledge that life is not always supposed to be pleasurable.

Facebook site: Friends and Family of Those Suffering From Addiction. April 23, 2016. This article was adapted by them with permission from the Harvard Mental Health Letter and Overcoming Addiction: Paths toward recovery, a special health report published by Harvard Health Publications.

BIBLIOGRAPHY

Holy Bible. *Translations: Life Application Study Bible, New Living Translation, King James Version, and The Message*

Source: U.S. Department of Health and Human Services. National Center for Health Statistics. Survey on Child Health. Washington, DC, 1993.

Facebook: Friends and Family of Those Suffering from Addiction April 23, 2016
Healthguide.org

Leaf, Dr. Caroline, <u>**Who Switched Off My Brain?**</u> Controlling Toxic Thoughts and Emotions **www.drleaf.com**

<u>**The Twelve Steps - A Spiritual Journey**</u> - A Working Guide for Adult Children from Addictive and Other Dysfunctional Families - Based on Biblical Teachings. Recovery Publications, Inc.

Keller, Timothy, **<u>Jesus the King,</u>** <u>Understanding the Life and Death of the Son of God</u>

"Alarming New Stats on US Heroin Epidemic", ***www.Medscape.com***, Monday October 10, 2016

"National Survey of Drug Use and Health", **National Institute on Drug Abuse, www.drugabuse.gov**

Lewis, C.S., **<u>The Chronicles of Narnia: The Lion, the Witch, and the Wardrobe,</u>** Harper Collins, NY NY

<u>Living in Freedom Every Day</u>, Faith Christian Family Church, Truesdale, MO

<u>www.CDC/Addiction</u>

SUGGESTED RESOURCES

The Holy Bible. 66 Books. Published by God.

The Twelve Steps - A Spiritual Journey. Published by Recovery Publications, Inc.

Beattie, Melody. **Codependent No More**. New York, N.Y. Harper Collins Publishers

Leaf, Dr. Caroline, **Who Switched Off My Brain?** www.drleaf.com

Bevere, James **The Bait of Satan,** Charisma House, 2014

Bevere, James **Breaking Intimidation,** Charisma House 2005

Stanley, Charles**, The Gift of Forgiveness,** Thomas Nelson Publisher, 2002

Meyer, Joyce **Word Name Blood,** Harrison House, Tulsa, OK

www.Celebraterecovery.com, 12 Step Christian Based Recovery, Find a CR Group near you

Facebook: Friends and Family of Those Suffering from Addiction

Alcoholics Anonymous The Big Book, World Services Inc. NY NY

Manning, Brendan, **The Ragamuffin Gospel,** Multnomah Publishers, Sisters, Oregon

Prince, Joseph, **Destined to Reign,** Harrison House 2010

Lewis, C.S., **The Lion, The Witch, and the Wardrobe, The Chronicles of Narnia,** Harper House, NY NY

Living in Freedom Every Day, Faith Christian Family Church, Truesdale, MO

Roberts, Terry, **A Healthy Christian Life,** Faith Christian Family Church, Truesdale, MO

30608155R00142

Made in the USA
Lexington, KY
11 February 2019